Revise
Edexcel GCSE
English
Student Workbook

Keith Hurst
Racheal Smith

A PEARSON COMPANY

Contents

Introduction	4

English Unit 2 | Section A: Shakespeare

Lesson 1 Answering a question on character	6
ResultsPlus Build better answers	12
Lesson 2 Answering questions on performance	14
ResultsPlus Build better answers	20
Lesson 3 Answering questions on themes in Shakespeare	22
ResultsPlus Build better answers	28

English Unit 2 | Section B: Different Cultures

Lesson 4 Answering character questions	30
ResultsPlus Build better answers	36
Lesson 5 Answering questions on language	38
ResultsPlus Build better answers	44
Lesson 6 Answering questions on theme and context	46
ResultsPlus Build better answers	52

English Unit 2 | Section C: Writing

Lesson 7 Making the right decisions	54
ResultsPlus Build better answers	60
Lesson 8 Choosing the right word	62
ResultsPlus Build better answers	68
Lesson 9 Choosing sentences	70
ResultsPlus Build better answers	76
Lesson 10 Making best use of paragraphs	78
ResultsPlus Build better answers	84

Introduction

This Workbook is designed to help you focus your revision and provide support as you prepare for your Edexcel GCSE English examination.

Some students think that there is no need to revise for English examinations. This is simply not true! By making yourself familiar with the type of questions being asked and the mark schemes used by the examiner, you will increase your chances of performing to your full potential in the examination.

How to improve your revision technique

1 The first thing to do is to make use of your teacher, as they are a very valuable resource! Listen carefully to all the revision guidance and tips your teacher gives you in lesson time. If there is something you are unsure about, remember to ask. Your teacher may hold extra revision classes at lunchtime in the run-up to the examinations. If so, make sure you take advantage of this opportunity.

2 Check that you are familiar with what the examination papers look like, how many marks are awarded to each question and how much time you will have in each examination. There is guidance on this provided opposite.

3 The most effective way to revise is through active strategies. This means:
   - practising the skills you have acquired throughout the course
   - taking part in completing revision activities to consolidate your knowledge
   - comparing your answers with sample answers to see exactly where you can improve your performance. You can do this using this Workbook.

Using the Revise Edexcel GCSE English Student Workbook

This Workbook has been written to help you to revise the skills and knowledge that you will have covered in your GCSE English course. You may work through the book with your teacher within lessons. However, the activities in the Workbook are also suitable for you to complete during your own independent revision time.

It has been designed for you to revise actively. There is room for you to write answers to activities and practise the skills required by completing sample examination questions. You are encouraged to highlight and annotate examination questions and texts as you might do in the examination itself.

The book is divided into three parts to reflect the three Sections of the Unit 2 English examination. The tops of the pages are colour-coded to make it clear which part you are in.

As a reminder, here is a summary of the requirements for each Section of the examination:

English Unit 2: The Writer's Craft		
Time allowed		**Text allowed?**
2 hours	**Section A: Shakespeare**	No
	Section B: Different Cultures Prose	
	Section C: Writing	

Introduction

The following are some of the features that make this Workbook as user-friendly as possible:

- The lesson **introduction** will explain which part of the examination you will be revising for.
- **Learning objectives** at the start of each lesson explain what you will be aiming to achieve when answering this part of the examination.
- **ResultsPlus Build your skills** lists the skills you will be practising in the lesson and asks you to decide how confident you are with each of the skills listed – from red for 'not at all' to green for 'confident'. At the end of the lesson you will have the chance to review your confidence level again by filling in the same table. Your knowledge of the skills covered in the lesson should have improved.
- The **timer icon** gives a suggestion for how long you should spend on each activity. This is for guidance when working through the Workbook only - remember that this is not a suggestion for how long to spend on the examination question itself!
- **References** for extracts are included in this Workbook (e.g. chapter and page numbers) to allow you to look them up in your own copy and to re-inforce your knowledge of the text. These references are to the editions of the text which are listed as 'Prescribed texts' by Edexcel. Note that you will not be given a page reference for the extracts you are given in the examination question paper.
- **ResultsPlus Build better answers** give you an opportunity to read the mark schemes against which you will be assessed, and to match these to example student answers.

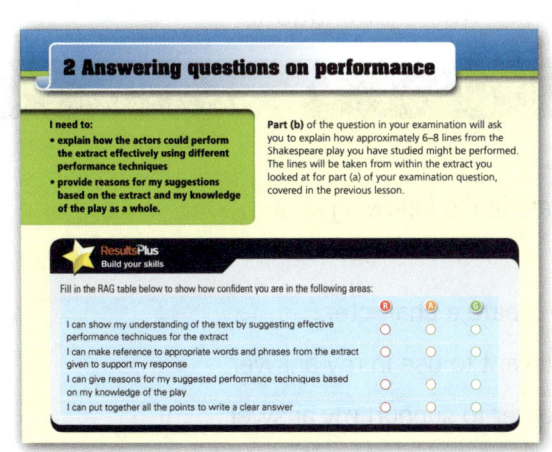

Finally, stay positive throughout your revision: think about what you can do, not what you can't. Good luck!

1 Answering a question on character

I need to:
- show that I understand a character
- recognise the techniques that writers use to create a character
- refer to relevant evidence from the extract to support my points.

In this section of the examination, you will be given a short extract from the play you have studied. **Part (a)** of the question will ask you to explain what you learn about a particular character from this extract. You will not be able to take a copy of the text you have studied into the examination.

ResultsPlus
Build your skills

Fill in the RAG table below to show how confident you are in the following areas:

	R	A	G
I can recognise the techniques that writers use to create a character	○	○	○
I can identify evidence from the extract which is relevant to use in my answer	○	○	○
I can comment effectively on evidence identified in order to support my answer	○	○	○
I can put together all the points to write a clear answer	○	○	○

Activity 1

You will need to know about how the characters in the play you have studied are portrayed in order to prepare for the examination question on an extract.

1 Read the description of either Macbeth (*Macbeth*) or Romeo (*Romeo and Juliet*) and use the words in the box to fill in the gaps. Look up any words you are unfamiliar with.

Romeo and Juliet

Romeo's role as a romantic lover is _____ and in general we feel sympathy towards him in the play. His love for Juliet is passionate. After he meets Juliet, he forgets Rosaline immediately. This shows that he is _____. He is a _____ friend to Mercutio. His attempts to make peace with Tybalt are _____. His decision to fight Tybalt shows he is _____ and _____. He rarely considers the consequences of his actions.

He is brave in fights but he is weak and _____ when he speaks to Friar Lawrence. His decision to get married to Juliet in secret shows that his feelings are _____. His decision to leave Verona and go into exile could be seen as _____.

> sincere   tragic   cowardly   fickle   desperate   loyal
> immature   well-intentioned   hot-headed

6

English Unit 2 | *Section A: Shakespeare*

Macbeth

Macbeth is an evil character and we generally feel _____ towards him in the play. He is a _____ fighter and is _____ by others. But the qualities he shows in times of war are not suitable for peacetime. He feels grateful towards Duncan at the start of the play because of his promotion, so his murder of the King is especially _____ . Although he likes to think of himself as _____ , his wife challenges him and wounds his _____ . This strengthens his resolve to kill Duncan.

He feels _____ after the murder of the King. He kills Banquo and Macduff's family to try to cover up his deed. This shows that he is _____ . Later in the play, Macbeth misinterprets the witches' predictions and this is a sign of his stupidity and _____ . His actions as King show he is only out to _____ himself.

| manly | threatened | treacherous | brave | ruthless | admired |
| arrogance | pride | protect | disgust |

2 How far do you agree with the description of the character from the text you have studied? Do you think the words used are appropriate? For any that you disagree with, rewrite the sentence or phrase below using more appropriate words and give a reason for your change, using evidence from the play.

New sentence:

Reason for change:

New sentence:

Reason for change:

7

1 Answering a question on character

Activity 2

20 MINS

1 Find the extract specified for your chosen play and answer the questions below. This will help you to think about how the characters are presented, but you won't get questions like this in your examination.

Romeo and Juliet, Act 3, Scene 1

Look at **Act 3, Scene 1**. Read the section halfway through this scene from Mercutio's exit after he has been stabbed, to Romeo's exit after he has killed Tybalt.

The extract begins...

Romeo	This gentleman, the Prince's near ally,
	My very friend, hath got this mortal hurt
	...
Romeo	O, I am fortune's fool!
Benvolio	Why dost thou stay? ***Exit ROMEO***

... and ends

a Romeo says that his reputation has been 'stain'd with Tybalt's slander'. What did Tybalt say that upset Romeo so much? Why did this upset him?

_____
_____
_____

b Why does Romeo say that Juliet's beauty 'hath made me effeminate'?

_____
_____
_____

c What does Romeo mean when he says 'This day's black fate on more days doth depend'? What does this tell us about him?

_____
_____
_____

d 'Away to heaven, respective lenity, / And fire-eyed fury be my conduct now!' How does Romeo intend to change his behaviour?

_____
_____
_____

e Romeo says 'I am fortune's fool!' What does this mean and what does it tell us about him?

_____
_____
_____

English Unit 2 | Section A: Shakespeare

Look at **Act 2, Scene 3**. Read the section towards the end of the scene from Macbeth's return from seeing Duncan's body, to when Lady Macbeth faints.

The extract begins…

> **Macbeth** Had I but died an hour before this chance
> I had lived a blessèd time…
> …
> **Macbeth** …Who could refrain,
> That had a heart to love – and in that heart
> Courage, to make's love known?

… and ends

a Macbeth says 'Had I but died an hour before this chance, / I had lived a blessèd time.' What does he mean? Is he being sincere?

_____
_____
_____

b Macbeth comments that 'The wine of life is drawn, and the mere lees is left.' What is Macbeth saying about Duncan's death? Does he mean what he says?

_____
_____
_____

c Macbeth announces Duncan's death to his son Donalbain. What do you think of the way he does this?

_____
_____
_____

d Is Macbeth lying completely when he talks of being 'loyal' and feeling 'love' for Duncan?

_____
_____
_____

e Macduff asks Macbeth why he killed Duncan's attendants. He might be suspicious of Macbeth. What do you think of Macbeth's explanation?

_____
_____
_____

Macbeth, Act 2, Scene 3

1 Answering a question on character

Activity 3

To do well in part (a) of this section of the examination, it is important that you:

- have a good understanding of the main characters in the play as a whole so that you are able to comment effectively on how a character is presented within the extract you are given in the examination.

- make *at least* three separate points which show your understanding of how the character is presented within the extract

- support each point with relevant evidence from the extract. This evidence may be in the form of a short quotation or a reference to something that is shown in the extract.

You won't know in advance which character you will be asked to write about but you will know the Act from which the extract is taken and the stem of the question will not change.

1. Answer the sample examination question below about the play you are studying, using the extract you looked at in Activity 2. Choose the question for the tier that you are going to be entered for (check with your teacher if you're not sure).

Romeo and Juliet

Foundation Tier

From the extract, what do you learn about the character of Romeo?

Use **evidence** from the extract to support your answer. (7 marks)

Higher Tier

Explain how Shakespeare presents the character of Romeo in the extract.

Use **evidence** from the extract to support your answer. (7 marks)

Macbeth

Foundation Tier

From the extract, what do you learn about the character of Macbeth?

Use **evidence** from the extract to support your answer. (7 marks)

Higher Tier

Explain how Shakespeare presents the character of Macbeth in the extract.

Use **evidence** from the extract to support your answer. (7 marks)

To help get you started you might want to look back at your answers to Activity 2. Here are some tips for writing a good answer:

- Remember what you already know about the character and their personality. This will help you make more subtle points.

- Make sure you have evidence from the extract to back up all your points.

- Think carefully when choosing evidence from the extract. There may be more than one word or phrase you can use as evidence – choose the best ones!

- It is crucial that you explain why the evidence proves your point.

English Unit 2 | *Section A: Shakespeare*

Try to look at a clean copy of the extract specified in Activity 2 – remember that you won't be allowed your own copy of the text within your examination! You will, however, be given a clean copy of the extract that is set.

ResultsPlus
Build better answers

1. Look back at the question you answered for Activity 3. Read the extract below or opposite from the student response relevant to your text and tier.

2. Using the mark scheme opposite, decide which band the answer would achieve. Give a reason for your decision.

I think the student would obtain a Band _____ because _____

_____

Romeo and Juliet

Student A: Foundation Tier

Romeo is angry because Tybalt has killed Mercutio and insulted him. He has tried to be friendly to Tybalt because Tybalt is related to Juliet who is now his wife, but Tybalt has killed his friend Mercutio and Romeo is really angry. He has 'fire-eyed fury' and this shows he wants to get his own back on Tybalt.

Student B: Higher Tier

Romeo is upset because all his rather naïve hopes for peace as a result of his marriage have been destroyed and his friend Mercutio has 'got his mortal hurt'.

Rather than question his own behaviour, Romeo talks of 'this day's black fate' and he seems to welcome the feelings of anger that overwhelm him, instead of resisting them in a mature way. He feels that his love for Juliet has made him 'effeminate' and he is irate because Tybalt is showing off 'in triumph'.

When Tybalt calls him 'wretched boy', it seems to question Romeo's manhood so he feels that he has to fight to prove himself. After he has killed Tybalt, he calls himself 'fortune's fool' which suggests that he doesn't take responsibility for his actions.

Macbeth

Student A: Foundation Tier

Macbeth is surrounded by people who have just discovered Duncan's body and who must be feeling all kinds of emotions at the murder of their king and father. Macbeth must be careful not to give himself away and needs to keep calm.

So Macbeth has to put on an act. He pretends he is devastated by Duncan's death and wishes he has 'died an hour before this chance'. He has also killed the King's grooms in an attempt to lay the blame on them. When Macduff questions why he did it, Macbeth shows he can be clever as he says it was because he was angry and loved Duncan so much.

Student B: Higher Tier

The events in this extract test Macbeth's ability to 'look like the innocent flower but be the serpent under it'. He has to tread a delicate balance between showing sorrow for Duncan's death and not over-exaggerating his grief. So his speech is measured, grave and dignified: 'there's nothing serious in mortality'. Perhaps Macbeth is demonstrating the statesmanlike leadership qualities that will make him seem suitable as king.

Macbeth is cunning enough to turn his killing of the King's chamberlains to his own advantage. He presents the deed as evidence of his love and loyalty towards Duncan ('who could refrain that had a heart to love'). It is also poignant and ironic because we know Macbeth did have a reason to love and be loyal to Duncan.

Foundation Tier

Band	Description
1	• Basic understanding of the character. • Limited reference to the extract to support response
2	• Some understanding of the character • Some reference to the extract to support response
3	• Generally sound or sound understanding of the character • Clear reference to the extract to support response

Higher Tier

Band	Description
1	• Generally sound or sound understanding of the character • Clear reference to the extract to support response
2	• Thorough understanding of the character • Sustained reference to the extract to support response
3	• Perceptive understanding of the character • Discriminating reference to the extract to support response

ResultsPlus
Build your skills

Fill in the RAG table below to see how your confidence has improved in the following areas:

	R	A	G
I can recognise the techniques that writers use to create a character	○	○	○
I can identify evidence from the extract which is relevant to use in my answer	○	○	○
I can comment effectively on evidence identified in order to support my answer	○	○	○
I can put together all the points to write a clear answer	○	○	○

2 Answering questions on performance

I need to:
- explain how the actors could perform the extract effectively using different performance techniques
- provide reasons for my suggestions based on the extract and my knowledge of the play as a whole.

Part (b) of the question in your examination will ask you to explain how approximately 6–8 lines from the Shakespeare play you have studied might be performed. The lines will be taken from within the extract you looked at for part (a) of your examination question, covered in the previous lesson.

ResultsPlus
Build your skills

Fill in the RAG table below to show how confident you are in the following areas:

	R	A	G
I can show my understanding of the text by suggesting effective performance techniques for the extract	○	○	○
I can make reference to appropriate words and phrases from the extract given to support my response	○	○	○
I can give reasons for my suggested performance techniques based on my knowledge of the play	○	○	○
I can put together all the points to write a clear answer	○	○	○

Activity 1

1. Read the extract from the play you have studied that follows. It shows the opening lines from the extract you looked at in Lesson 1.

2. Complete the sentences that follow the extract. This will help you to think about the context of the extract and the thoughts and feelings of the characters who feature in it. Remember that you won't get questions like this within your examination.

Romeo and Juliet, Act 3, Scene 1

Romeo   This gentleman, the Prince's near ally,
My very friend, hath got this mortal hurt
In *my* behalf: my reputation stained
With Tybalt's slander. —Tybalt! — that an hour
Hath been my cousin. O sweet Juliet —
Thy beauty hath made me effeminate
And in my temper softened valour's steel!

English Unit 2 | Section A: Shakespeare

Macbeth, Act 2, Scene 3

Macbeth Had I but died an hour before this chance,
I had lived a blessèd time – for, from this instant,
There's nothing serious in mortality.
All is but toys: renown and grace is dead —
The wine of life is drawn, and the mere lees
Is left this vault to brag of.

a The setting of this extract is _____

b The event(s) which have taken place before this point are _____

_____

_____

c The mood at this point of the play is _____

d Romeo's/Macbeth's three main emotions (how he feels) at this point are

1 _____

2 _____

3 _____

e Romeo's/Macbeth's main overall objective (what he wants to achieve) at this point in

the play is _____

_____

_____

2 Answering questions on performance

If you are taking the Foundation Tier paper, you will be given a list of the areas of performance you might want to think about when writing your answer. These are:

- actions
- positioning of actors
- movement
- voice
- gesture
- facial expression

If you are taking the Higher Tier paper, you will not be given this list, but these are the points you might want to think about in your answer.

Activity 2

1. Look at the lines from your play below. They are taken from the extract you looked at in Lesson 1. Highlight any words or phrases that will be relevant in thinking about the six areas of performance listed above.

Romeo and Juliet, Act 3, Scene 1

Benvolio	Romeo, away, be gone!
	The citizens are up, and Tybalt slain.
	Stand not amazed! The Prince will doom thee death
	If thou art taken. Hence, be gone, away!
Romeo	O, I am fortune's fool!
Benvolio	Why dost thou stay?

Exit ROMEO

Macbeth, Act 2, Scene 3

Macbeth	O, yet I do repent me of my fury –
	That I did kill them.
Macduff	Wherefore did you so?
Macbeth	Who can be wise, amazed, temperate and furious,
	Loyal and neutral, in a moment? No man!

English Unit 2 | *Section A: Shakespeare*

2 Fill in the table below to suggest how these lines could be performed. Look back at your answers to the questions in Activity 1 – they will help you to think about the reasons you need to include to support your answer. One example has been completed for you.

Word or phrase from the extract	Possible performance technique	Reasons for suggestion
Romeo, away, be gone!	Romeo has dropped to his knees over the body of Tybalt	Romeo is shocked by the fact that he has just killed Tybalt in a fit of rage at Mercutio's death. He is overwhelmed by a feeling of disbelief and therefore does not move from the stage.
O, yet I do repent me of my fury	Macbeth covers his face with his hands.	Macbeth has to convince Macduff and all the others present that he is horrified and truly upset at the death of Duncan and ashamed that he has killed Duncan's guards. Covering his face helps to disguise his expression which might give his true feelings away.

17

2 Answering questions on performance

Activity 3

20 MINS

In this activity you will practise answering part (b) of a sample examination question yourself.

Look at the sample examination question below. It refers to the extract printed on page 16 you looked at in Activity 2.

> Using your understanding of the extract, explain how the following lines from the extract might be performed.
>
> Give reasons for your answer. (7 marks)

1. Before you start writing your response, look back at your responses to Activities 1 and 2, and jot down a plan for your writing in the space below, based on these answers.

   In addition, if you can, think about:

   - how each character relates to other characters at this point in the play and how this affects their movements, gestures and positioning;
   - how their behaviour might change between the start of the extract and the end;
   - how a character might behave when they're silent (have no lines to speak).

   Bear in mind that you will **not** have to make reference to how a character will use stage props or stage furniture.

2 Now write your complete answer to the question opposite. Remember to focus your response on the 5-8 lines you have been given (in this example, those on page 16). You will not be allowed a copy of your set text within the examination.

ResultsPlus
Build better answers

Below and opposite are extracts from student answers to the part (b) sample examination question you looked at in Activity 3.

1 Read the extract from the student response that is relevant to your text and tier. Using the mark schemes opposite, decide which band you think the answer would achieve. Give reasons for your decision.

I think the student would obtain a Band _____ because _____

_____

Romeo and Juliet

Student A: Foundation Tier

Romeo will be out of breath because he has just fought with Tybalt and killed him. He was very angry because Tybalt killed Mercutio and he is just starting to calm down. He doesn't know what to do so Benvolio has to tell him that the prince will execute him for what he has done. Benvolio shouts at him because there are exclamation marks and Romeo is standing paralysed.

Student B: Higher Tier

Romeo has just killed Tybalt in a fit of rage but is realising the enormity of what he has done. He should drop his sword and drop to his knees in a kind of trance (Benvolio urges him to 'stand not amaz'd').

Benvolio is much more quick-thinking. His first two lines should be called across to Romeo (who is centre stage) from the side of the stage where he is keeping an eye on the approaching crowd — 'the citizens are up' and coming towards them. Then he should rush to Romeo and drag him to his feet. He shouts the next line about the prince into Romeo's face and he holds on to Romeo's shoulders to try to get the message across.

Romeo should seem sorry for himself and should shout out his line with the emphasis on 'fool'.

Macbeth

Student A: Foundation Tier

Macbeth has just come from the king's bedroom where the king's body is and he has just killed the king's guards. He is trying to get everybody to believe the guards killed the king but Macduff thinks it was a funny thing to do.

He has all these people standing around watching him so he must not let on that he has done anything wrong. I bet Lady Macbeth is worried about this because she's in this scene too. Macbeth has to put on an act of being upset about the king. He asks a rhetorical question and answers it himself.

Student B: Higher Tier

> Macbeth tells us that he has killed the grooms. This is a shock to the audience because it wasn't planned and it is a shock to everyone on stage, too. Macbeth needs to be careful how he announces this so he pauses between 'fury' and 'That I did kill them'. He could say his first line looking into the heavens and his second line facing the other characters on stage. Most of the characters on stage will react to the announcement with surprise, although Malcolm and Donalbain are probably more concerned about their own grief and may be comforting each other. Lady Macbeth will react differently — she will be surprised at first but will realise Macbeth's actions were sensible and might even allow herself a quiet smile.

Foundation Tier

Band	Description
1	• Basic understanding of effectiveness of performance techniques • Limited reference to the lines from the extract to support response
2	• Occasional understanding of effectiveness of performance techniques • Some reference to the lines from the extract to support response
3	• Generally sound or sound understanding of effectiveness of performance techniques • Clear reference to the lines from the extract to support response

Higher Tier

Band	Description
1	• Generally sound or sound understanding of effectiveness of performance techniques • Clear reference to the lines from the extract to support response
2	• Thorough understanding of effectiveness of performance techniques • Sustained reference to the lines from the extract to support response
3	• Perceptive understanding of effectiveness of performance techniques • Discriminating reference to the lines from the extract to support response

ResultsPlus
Build your skills

Fill in the RAG table below to see how your confidence has improved in the following areas:

	R	A	G
I can show my understanding of the text by suggesting effective performance techniques for this extract	○	○	○
I can make reference to appropriate words and phrases from the extract to support my response	○	○	○
I can give reasons for my suggested performance techniques based on my knowledge of the play	○	○	○
I can put together all the points to write a clear answer	○	○	○

3 Answering questions on themes in Shakespeare

I need to:
- show that I understand the key themes within the play
- comment on the importance of a theme within a chosen section of the play.

Part (c) of the question in Section A of your examination will ask you to choose a section of the play you have studied that relates to a specific theme. You will need to choose a section of the play that presents this theme and write an answer commenting on its importance or significance in the part of the play you have chosen.

ResultsPlus
Build your skills

Fill in the RAG table below to show how confident you are in the following areas:

	R	A	G
I am aware of the major themes within the play	○	○	○
I can choose an appropriate section of the play which relates to a given theme	○	○	○
I can comment on the significance or importance of the theme within my chosen section of the play	○	○	○
I can make references to the section of the play I have chosen in order to support my response	○	○	○

Activity 1

10 MINS

Broadly, a theme is an idea about life which a writer is presenting. While the play deals with events, such as Romeo's killing of Tybalt, these events provide evidence of the play's themes, such as revenge, conflict or fate.

1. Identify as many themes within the play you have studied as you can, and list them in the table opposite. An example has been given to start you off.

2. In the second column of the table, write down one key example of an event from each act that tells us something about each theme. You should try to do this from memory – remember, you won't have the text available in the examination! If you can't remember the Act and Scene in which the event takes place, try to describe it as fully as possible.

English Unit 2 | *Section A: Shakespeare*

	Theme	Sections of the play that tell us about this theme
Romeo and Juliet	Love	The last section of Act 2, Scene 2 — just after Romeo and Juliet have met for the first time. The beginning of Act 3, Scene 5 — the lovers' final parting.
Macbeth	Power	The beginning of Act 5 Scene 3 — Macbeth's misuse of power is causing his people to desert him and his mistreatment of the messenger further shows him to be a tyrant.

23

3 Answering questions on themes in Shakespeare

Activity 2

1 Now take one of the themes you identified in Activity 1. Concentrating on just one of the parts of the play you identified for this theme, write at least three bullet points to explain how the theme and its importance is presented in this part of the play. An example has been given to help you. This exercise will help you to practise planning a response to a part (c) question.

Romeo and Juliet

Love: Act 2, Scene 2

- In the last section of this scene, the two lovers find it hard to part, which shows that each will find it difficult to live without the other.
- Shakespeare uses bird imagery throughout the last part of the scene. Juliet sees herself as the owner of a bird (Romeo) to whom she does not want to give freedom. She is 'loving-jealous of his liberty' and this shows that love is partly selfish.
- The lovers agree to meet at nine o'clock the next day but Romeo thinks it will seem like a twenty-year wait. It is clear that the lovers' absence from each other will be painful.

Macbeth

Power: Act 5, Scene 3

- At the beginning of this scene, Macbeth has been told that some of his men are deserting him. This shows that he has not been a popular leader and he has abused his power.
- Macbeth believes he will never lose his power because he believes what the witches have told him. But he is hanging on to power for its own sake.
- He insults the messenger who brings him news, even before he has let him speak. This shows he uses his powerful position to be disrespectful to others.

3 Answering questions on themes in Shakespeare

Activity 3

20 MINS

Look again at the extract you wrote about in Lesson 1 on pages 8–9. Below is an example of the type of question you will get in part (c) of Section A of your examination for which you will have to choose your own extract. Read the question that is relevant to your text and tier.

Romeo and Juliet

Foundation Tier

In the extract, Romeo speaks of 'black fate'.

Comment on how fate is important in **one other** part of the play. (10 marks)

Higher Tier

In the extract, Romeo speaks of 'black fate'.

Explore the significance of fate in **one other** part of the play. (10 marks)

Macbeth

Foundation Tier

In the extract, Macbeth speaks of violence.

Comment on how Macbeth's use of violence is important in **one other** part of the play. (10 marks)

Higher Tier

In the extract, Macbeth speaks of violence.

Explore the significance of the use of violence in **one other** part of the play. (10 marks)

1 Choose an extract from the play other than the extract on pages 8–9 in which we see the importance of the theme and write your response to the sample examination question. You should try to comment on how this theme is important to understanding this part of the play if you are answering the Higher Tier question.

English Unit 2 | *Section A: Shakespeare*

ResultsPlus
Build better answers

Below and opposite are extracts from student answers to the part (c) sample examination question you looked at in Activity 3.

1 Read the extracts from the student response that is relevant to your text and tier. Using the mark schemes opposite, decide which band you think each answer would achieve. Give reasons for your decision.

I think the student would obtain a Band _____ because _____

Romeo and Juliet

Student A: Foundation Tier

One important bit of fate in the play is in the last act when Friar Lawrence's letter to Romeo doesn't get through because Friar John was held up on the way to Mantua and Romeo had already left to go back to Verona because Balthasar has just told him that Juliet is dead.

If the letter had got through then Romeo would know that Juliet's death was faked. But he decides to commit suicide to be with her in spirit and this is a sad waste because both of them could have lived. Romeo says 'I defy you stars' which reminds us that they are 'star-crossed lovers' and have to die so that the Montagues and the Capulets will see how stupid they are and make peace.

Student B: Higher Tier

In the Prologue, the Chorus tells us exactly what is going to happen. The Capulets and the Montagues have 'an ancient grudge' and Romeo and Juliet have been born from 'the fatal loins' of these two opposing families. They are 'star-crossed lovers' who will lose their lives but their sacrifice will 'bury their parents' strife'. In other words, Shakespeare is using the play to communicate a very strong moral message: that unreserved love and laying down your life can overcome seemingly irreconcilable differences. This sacrifice is the destiny of the young couple, but Shakespeare's story of the pain and subsequent death of the lovers is poignant because it is wasteful, even though unavoidable.

Macbeth

Student A: Foundation Tier

Macbeth uses violence all through the play. The part I am going to talk about is when he kills Duncan in Act 2. This is important because it is the start of all Macbeth's troubles. Macbeth doesn't want to kill Duncan. The witches put the idea in his mind and then his wife gets to work on him, insulting his manhood, which affects Macbeth a lot because he is very proud. So when he finally kills Duncan he is on a downward spiral. He has to cover his tracks when people are suspicious of what he has done. He can't go back in time — he has to wade through a sea of blood from now on.

Student B: Higher Tier

> Macbeth uses violence in the final scene of the play, when he is fighting for his life. Macbeth is clearly a very good fighter and he is much admired at the start of the play for being brave in battle when he split his enemy 'from the nave to the chops'. However, he spends most of the play sneakily killing people who stand in his way. He murders Duncan in his sleep, he sends murderers to ambush Banquo, then he has Macduff's wife and children killed.
>
> At the end of the play he has almost nothing left to fight for but he will not give up. Shakespeare shows at the end that Macbeth has some of the qualities of bravery and dignity that he had at the beginning. If it wasn't for his violence due to ambition, his wife and the witches he could have been a much better person.

Foundation Tier

Band	Description
1	• Basic understanding of theme and its importance • Limited reference to one other part of the play to support response
2	• Some understanding of theme and its importance • Some reference to one other part of the play to support response
3	• Generally sound or sound understanding of theme and its importance • Clear reference to one other part of the play to support response

Higher Tier

Band	Description
1	• Generally sound or sound understanding of theme and its importance • Clear reference to one other part of the play to support response
2	• Thorough understanding of theme and its importance • Sustained reference to one other part of the play to support response
3	• Perceptive understanding of theme and its importance • Discriminating reference to one other part of the play to support response

ResultsPlus
Build your skills

Fill in the RAG table below to see how your confidence has improved in the following areas:

	R	A	G
I am aware of the major themes within the play	○	○	○
I can choose an appropriate section of the play which relates to a given theme	○	○	○
I can comment on the significance or importance of the theme within my chosen section of the play	○	○	○
I can make references to the section of the play I have chosen in order to support my response	○	○	○

4 Answering character questions

I need to:
- show that I understand the characters
- refer to relevant examples from the extract to support my points.

In this section of the examination, you will be given a short extract from the text you have studied. **Part (a)** of the question will ask you to explain what this extract tells you about a key character. You will not be able to take a copy of your text into the examination.

ResultsPlus
Build your skills

Fill in the RAG table below to show how confident you are in the following areas:

	R	A	G
I can recognise the techniques that writers use to create a character	○	○	○
I can identify evidence from the extract which is relevant to use in my answer	○	○	○
I can comment effectively on evidence identified in order to support my answer	○	○	○

Activity 1

10 MINS

You will need to know how the characters in the novel you have studied are portrayed in order to prepare for this examination question. This exercise will help to review your knowledge.

1 Answer the following questions about the character George in *Of Mice and Men* or Scout in *To Kill a Mockingbird*. There may be more than one answer – tick all boxes that are relevant. Each time, you should write down a piece of evidence from the novel that supports your answer.

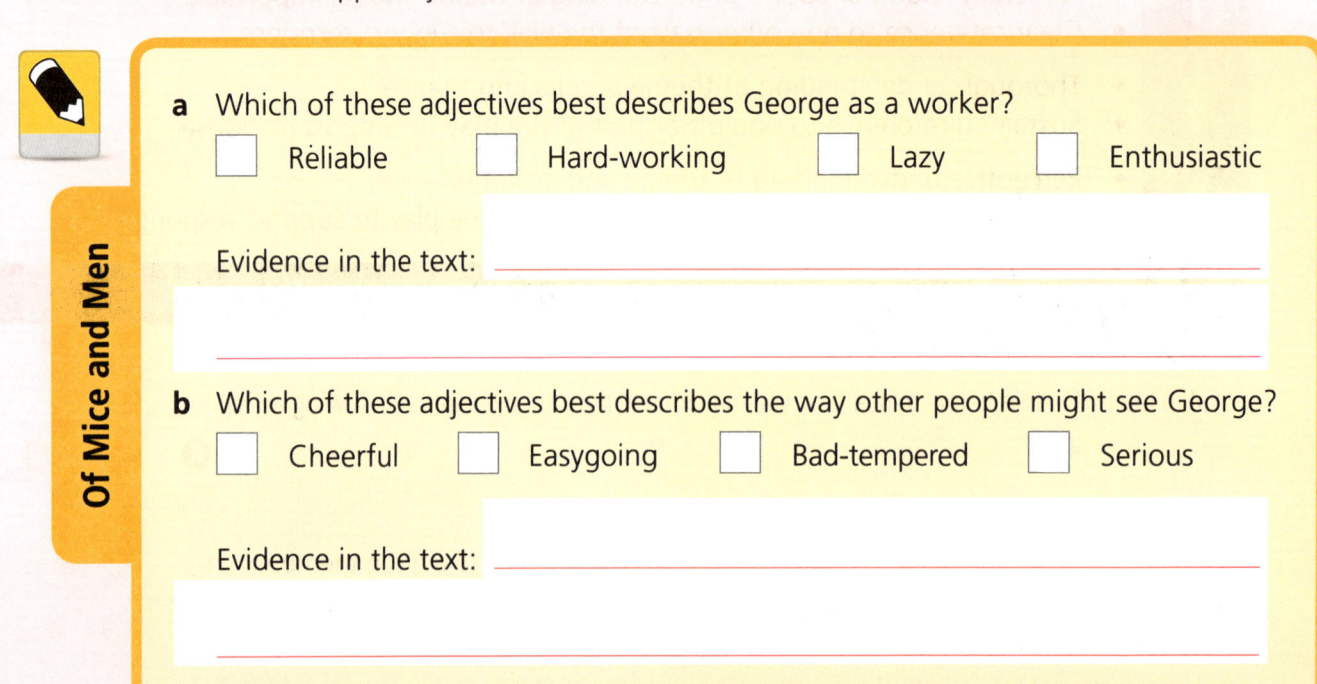

Of Mice and Men

a Which of these adjectives best describes George as a worker?

☐ Reliable ☐ Hard-working ☐ Lazy ☐ Enthusiastic

Evidence in the text: _____

b Which of these adjectives best describes the way other people might see George?

☐ Cheerful ☐ Easygoing ☐ Bad-tempered ☐ Serious

Evidence in the text: _____

30

English Unit 2 | *Section B: Different Cultures*

c Which of these best describes the way George behaves?

☐ Forgetful ☐ Plans ahead ☐ Avoids difficult decisions ☐ He never enjoys himself

Evidence in the text: _____

d Which of these words best describes the way George treats Lennie?

☐ Caring ☐ Cruel ☐ Protective ☐ Indifferent

Evidence in the text: _____

To Kill a Mockingbird

a Which of these best describes Scout's behaviour as a young girl?

☐ A tomboy ☐ Feminine and ladylike ☐ Obedient ☐ Independent

Evidence in the text: _____

b Which of these phrases best describes Scout's attitude towards education?

☐ Reluctant learner ☐ Listens carefully to adults ☐ Wants to do her own thing ☐ Feels superior to other children

Evidence in the text: _____

c Which of these words best describes Scout as a friend?

☐ Loyal ☐ Bossy ☐ Selfish ☐ Caring

Evidence in the text: _____

d Which of these phrases best describes what Scout feels about Jem?

☐ Frustrated by him ☐ Admires him ☐ Confused by him ☐ Relies on him

Evidence in the text: _____

31

4 Answering character questions

Activity 2

15 MINS

1 Read the extract below and highlight all the words and/or phrases that tell us something about the character of George or Scout.

2 Then answer the questions that follow to help you think about the effect of the language. Remember that you won't get questions like this on the extract in your exam.

Of Mice and Men Section 2, pages 27–28

> His glance was at once calculating and pugnacious. Lennie squirmed under the look and shifted his feet nervously. Curley stepped gingerly close to him.
> 'You the new guys the old man was waitin' for?'
> 'We just come in,' said George.
> 'Let the big guy talk.'
> Lennie twisted with embarrassment.
> George said, 'S'pose he don't want to talk?'
> Curley lashed his body around. 'By Christ, he's gotta talk when he's spoke to. What the hell are you gettin' into it for?'
> 'We travel together,' said George coldly.
> 'Oh, so it's that way.'
> George was tense, and motionless. 'Yeah, it's that way.'
> Lennie was looking helplessly to George for instruction.
> 'An' you won't let the big guy talk, is that it?'
> 'He can talk if he wants to tell you anything.' He nodded slightly to Lennie.
> 'We jus' come in,' said Lennie softly.

a What does George's question 'S'pose he don't want to talk?' tell us about his attitude to Lennie?

_____
_____
_____

b What do we learn about George from the line 'George was tense, and motionless. "Yeah, it's that way."'? What does this tell us about his attitude to Curley?

_____
_____
_____

c Why does George '[nod] slightly to Lennie' when he says 'He can talk if he wants to tell you anything'?

_____
_____
_____

English Unit 2 | *Section B: Different Cultures*

To Kill a Mockingbird Chapter 28, pages 267–268

> Jem knew as well as I that it was difficult to walk fast without stumping a toe, tripping on stones, and other inconveniences, and I was barefooted. Maybe it was the wind rustling the trees. But there wasn't any wind and there weren't any trees except the big oak.
>
> Our company shuffled and dragged his feet, as if wearing heavy shoes. Whoever it was wore thick cotton pants; what I thought were trees rustling was the soft swish of cotton on cotton, wheek, wheek, with every step.
>
> I felt the sand go cold under my feet and I knew we were near the big oak. Jem pressed my head. We stopped and listened.
>
> Shuffle-foot had not stopped with us this time. His trousers swished softly and steadily. Then they stopped. He was running, running towards us with no child's steps.
>
> 'Run, Scout! Run! Run!' Jem screamed.

a What words or phrases show us that Scout is observant, intelligent and thinks things through carefully?

b What do the references to Jem tell us about Scout's relationship with him?

c What is there in Scout's choice of language that reveals aspects of her character? Pick out particular words or phrases and explain how they influence your view.

4 Answering character questions

Activity 3

15 MINS

To do well in part (a) of this section of the examination, it is important that you:

- have a good understanding of the main characters in the text as a whole so that you are able to comment effectively on how a character is presented within the extract you are given in the examination.
- make *at least* three separate points which show your understanding how the character is presented, based on evidence in the extract
- support each point with relevant evidence from the extract. This evidence may be in the form of a short quotation or single words in the extract.

You won't know in advance which character you will be asked to write about but the stem of the question will not change.

1 Read the sample examination question below that is relevant to your text and tier and write at least three paragraphs of your response in the space opposite.
If you are studying *Of Mice and Men*, look back at the extract on page 32. You might also want to comment on the text up to the words '"That's the boss's son,"' he said quietly' which can be found on page 28 in your copy of the text. If you are studying *To Kill a Mockingbird*, look back at the extract on page 33. You might also want to comment on the text up to the words '…sank into a flabby male stomach' which can be found on page 268 in your copy of the text.

Of Mice and Men

Foundation Tier

From this extract, what do you learn about the character George?

Use **evidence** from the extract to support your answer. (7 marks)

Higher Tier

Explain how the writer presents the character of George in this extract.

Use **evidence** from the extract to support your answer. (7 marks)

To Kill a Mockingbird

Foundation Tier

From this extract, what do you learn about the character Scout?

Use **evidence** from the extract to support your answer. (7 marks)

Higher Tier

Explain how the writer presents the character of Scout in this extract.

Use **evidence** from the extract to support your answer. (7 marks)

English Unit 2 | *Section B: Different Cultures*

To help get you started you might want to look back at your answers to Activity 2. Here are some tips for writing a good answer:

- Remember what you already know about the character and their personality. This will help you make more subtle points.
- Make sure you have evidence from the extract to back up all your points.
- Think carefully when choosing evidence from the extract. There may be more than one word or phrase you can use as evidence – choose the best ones!
- It is crucial that you explain why the evidence proves your point.

35

ResultsPlus
Build better answers

1 Look back at the question you answered for Activity 3. Read the student response to this question that is relevant to your text and tier.

20 MINS

Of Mice and Men

Student A: Foundation Tier

George is angry with Curley because Curley is nasty to them and rude. George doesn't show his anger, though, until Curley goes out then he says 'What the hell's he got on his shoulder?' He won't say that to Curley's face because Curley is the Boss's son.

Also, George doesn't want Lennie to speak because he knows Lennie is slow and dumb. He thinks Lennie will cause trouble like he did in Weed.

Student B: Higher Tier

George shows that he is very protective towards Lennie because he interrupts as soon as Curley asks Lennie a question. He is also sensitive to Lennie when Lennie 'squirmed with the look' and 'twisted with embarrassment'. George defends him by saying 'S'pose he don't want to talk'.

George also shows that he is dominant and can control Lennie. 'He nodded slowly to Lennie' to show that Lennie was allowed to speak.

To Kill a Mockingbird

Student A: Foundation Tier

Scout is a bit weak and feeble because she falls over when Jem tells her to run and she screams 'Jem, Jem, help me, Jem!'

She doesn't know what she is doing and panics and runs into the flabby male stomach. All the time she doesn't know who is attacking them but it's Bob Ewell.

Student B: Higher Tier

Scout is dressed as a ham and can't see or move very well but she is able to use her other senses to work out what is happening:

'Maybe it was the wind rustling the trees. But there wasn't any wind and there weren't any trees.'

This shows that she is observant and intelligent enough to work things out.

She respects Jem and understands him. The two of them know Scout can't move quickly without having to say anything about it ('Jem knew as well as I...'). She seems to know what is going through Jem's mind: 'Jem pressed my head. We stopped and listened.'

2 Using the mark schemes which appear below, decide which band the student's answer would achieve. Write an explanation of your decision.

Foundation Tier

Band	Description
1	• Basic understanding of the character • Limited reference to the extract to support response
2	• Some understanding of the character • Some reference to the extract to support response
3	• Generally sound or sound understanding of the character • Clear reference to the extract to support response

Higher Tier

Band	Description
1	• Generally sound or sound understanding of the character • Clear reference to the extract to support response
2	• Thorough understanding of the character • Sustained reference to the extract to support response
3	• Perceptive understanding of the character • Discriminating reference to the extract to support response

I think the student would obtain a Band _____ because _____

_____

3 Now look back at the answer to the examination question that you wrote in Activity 3. Use the mark schemes above to decide which band your answer would achieve and then write down two things you could do to improve your answer and achieve a mark in a higher band. You might want to look back at the bullet points on pages 34 and 35 to help you.

1 _____

2 _____

ResultsPlus
Build your skills

Fill in the RAG table below to see how your confidence has improved has improved in the following areas:

	R	A	G
I can recognise the techniques that writers use to create a character	○	○	○
I can identify evidence from the extract which is relevant to use in my answer	○	○	○
I can comment effectively on evidence identified in order to support my answer	○	○	○

5 Answering questions on language

I need to:
- show that I understand how the writer uses language to present ideas to the reader
- refer to relevant examples from the text to support my points.

Part (b) of Section B will ask you to write a short answer about the language used in an extract from the text you have studied. The question will be on how the writer uses language to present an idea, a relationship, a character's behaviour, attitude, thoughts or feelings. As you will see, what is being presented will vary from extract to extract but the focus will always be on how the writer uses language.

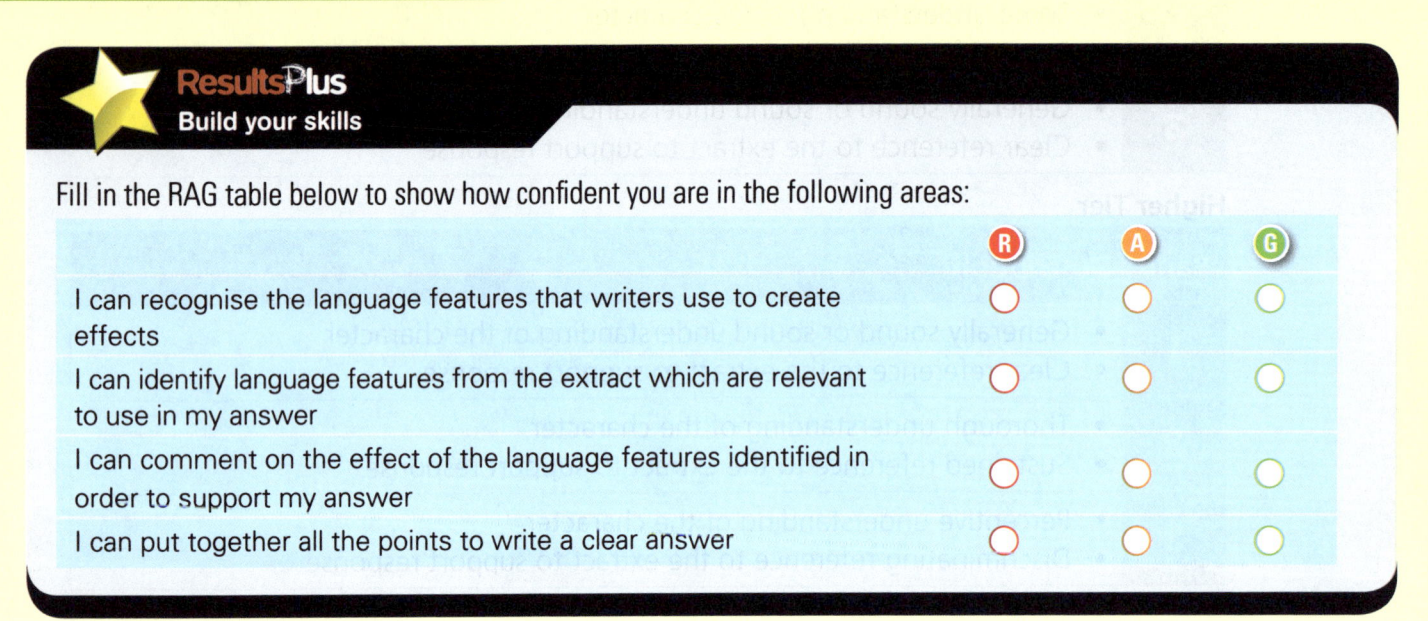

ResultsPlus — Build your skills

Fill in the RAG table below to show how confident you are in the following areas:

	R	A	G
I can recognise the language features that writers use to create effects	○	○	○
I can identify language features from the extract which are relevant to use in my answer	○	○	○
I can comment on the effect of the language features identified in order to support my answer	○	○	○
I can put together all the points to write a clear answer	○	○	○

Activity 1

10 MINS

1. Look at the definitions in the table on the opposite page. By choosing from the boxes below, select the language feature and example that goes with each definition. Write your answers in the table.

Language features

Noun	Personification
Verb	Simile
Adverb	Metaphor
Adjective	Colloquial language
Pronoun	Rhyme
Repetition	
Alliteration	

Examples

Quickly	As big as a bear
Run	The sun danced over the fields
She	The cold old farm
Green	The moggy is a goner
Rabbit	Snapped swiftly shut
	The darkest hour of the darkest night
	Her hair was silk

English Unit 2 | *Section B: Different Cultures*

	Definition	Language feature	Example
1	The name of a person, place or thing		
2	A word that gives us more information about a noun		
3	A word that gives us more information about a verb		
4	A word showing action, movement or being		
5	Takes the place of a noun so that you don't have to repeat it		
6	Using two or more words close together that begin with or include the same consonant		
7	Language showing how people speak		
8	Comparing two things using a word such as 'like' or 'as'		
9	A comparison where something is said to be something else, without using a word such as 'like'		
10	Describing things that are not human as if they were		
11	Using the same word or phrase more than once		
12	Patterns of similar sounds		

5 Answering questions on language

Activity 2

1 Read the extract from your chosen text below. A variety of language features have been highlighted. Can you name each one? Label each one on the extract. Remember that you will also need to comment on the effect of language features in your examination response, not simply identify features.

In this extract, Lennie is returning to the pool.

Of Mice and Men Section 6, page 109

> A far ==rush== of wind sounded and a gust drove through the tops of the trees ==like a wave==. The ==sycamore leaves turned up their silver sides==, the brown, dry leaves on the ground scudded a few feet. And row on row of tiny wind waves flowed up the pool's green surface.
>
> As quickly as it had come, the ==wind died==, and the clearing was quiet again. The heron stood in the shallows, motionless and waiting. Another little water snake swam up the pool, turning its ==periscope head== from side to side.
>
> Suddenly Lennie appeared out of the brush, and ==he came as silently as a creeping bear moves==. The heron ==pounded the air with its wings, jacked itself clear of the water and flew off down the river==. The little ==snake slid== in among the reeds at the pool's side.

In this extract, Scout and Jem are visiting Mrs Dubose.

To Kill a Mockingbird Chapter 11, pages 112–113

> She was horrible. Her face was the ==colour of a dirty pillow-case==, and the corners of her mouth glistened with wet, which ==inched like a glacier== down the deep grooves enclosing her chin. Old-age liver spots dotted her cheeks, and her ==pale eyes had black pinpoint pupils==. Her hands were knobbly, and the cuticles were grown up over finger-nails. Her bottom plate was not in, and her upper lip protruded; ==from time to time== she would draw her nether lip to her upper plate and carry her chin with it. This made the wet move faster.
>
> I didn't look any more than I had to. Jem reopened *Ivanhoe* and began reading. I tried to keep up with him, but he read too fast. When Jem came to a word he didn't know, he skipped it, but Mrs Dubose would catch him and make him spell it out. Jem read for perhaps twenty minutes, during which time I looked at the ==soot-stained== mantelpiece, out the window, anywhere to keep from looking at her. As he read along, I noticed that Mrs Dubose's corrections grew fewer and farther between, that Jem had even left ==one sentence dangling in mid-air==. She was not listening.

English Unit 2 | *Section B: Different Cultures*

In your answer to part (b) of the examination question, you will need to focus on the effect of the language features the writer uses and not simply identify the features.

You can write an effective response to a part (b) examination question by:

- firstly making a point, e.g.

> Lennie is portrayed by Steinbeck as a man who is closely linked to the natural world around him.

> Harper Lee is showing that, to Scout, this visit to Mrs Dubose appears to last a very long time.

- then picking out a suitable quotation and, if relevant, indentifying the language feature, e.g.

> This is shown by the simile 'Lennie … came as silently as a creeping bear moves'.

> The writer uses repetition in the phrase 'from time to time'.

- and finally explaining what effect the language feature creates, e.g.

> Steinbeck compares Lennie to a bear to suggest his strength and to show that he seems more at home in the woods, away from other humans.

> Harper Lee repeats the word 'time' to show how slow and drawn out the experience seems to be for Scout.

This structure is sometimes referred to as point, evidence and explanation (PEE).

2. Choose one of the highlighted quotations from the extract and write a brief explanation of the effect it creates in the reader's mind, using the PEE (point, evidence, explanation) structure.

41

5 Answering questions on language

Activity 3

20 MINS

1. Look at the sample examination question for your chosen text. Then read the extract specified, and think about examples of language you could use to answer this question.

Of Mice and Men Section 2, pages 27–28

Foundation Tier

Explain how the writer uses language to present Curley's behaviour in the extract.

Use **evidence** from the extract to support your answer. (7 marks)

Higher Tier

Comment on how language is used to present Curley's behaviour in the extract.

Use **evidence** from the extract to support your answer. (7 marks)

Below is the start of the extract you should use to answer this sample examination question. You used part of the same extract to practise answering a part (a) type question on pages 34–35. Make sure you look at the full extract which is on pages 27–28 of your copy of the text. It ends '"That's the boss's son,"' he said quietly.'

> At that moment a young man came into the bunk house; a thin young man with a brown face, with brown eyes and a head of tightly curled hair. He wore a work glove on his left hand, and, like the boss, he wore high-heeled boots. 'Seen my old man?' he asked.

To Kill a Mockingbird Chapter 28, pages 267–268

Foundation Tier

Explain how the writer uses language to present violence in this extract.

Use **evidence** from the text to support your answer. (7 marks)

Higher Tier

Comment on how language is used to present violence in the extract.

Use **evidence** from the extract to support your answer. (7 marks)

Below is the start of the extract you should use to answer this sample examination question. You used part of the same extract to practise answering a part (a) type question on pages 34-35. Make sure you look at the full extract which is on pages 267 – 268 of your copy of the text. It ends '…and sank into a flabby male stomach'.

> Jem knew as well as I that it was difficult to walk fast without stumping a toe, tripping on stones, and other inconveniences, and I was barefooted. Maybe it was the wind rustling the trees. But there wasn't any wind and there weren't any trees except the big oak.

3 Write a response to the examination question opposite, using the examples of language you have identified. Use the PEE model to help you.

ResultsPlus
Build better answers

1 Read the student response to the question from Activity 3 that is relevant to your text and tier. Using the mark schemes opposite, decide which band the answer would achieve. Write an explanation of your decision below.

I think the student would obtain a Band _____ because _____

_____

Of Mice and Men

Student A: Foundation Tier

Curley behaves in a mean way towards George and Lennie. The way he looks at them makes Lennie 'squirm'. He is angry when Lennie doesn't answer and George answers instead. 'Let the big guy talk.' He doesn't like big guys. 'By Christ, he's gotta talk when he's spoke to.'

Student B: Higher Tier

Right away, we see that Curley feels superior to the other men in the scene because 'like the boss, he wore high-heeled boots'. He also has 'tightly curled hair' which reflects his behaviour, as he is tense and seems ready to spring into action.

This superiority and tension are reflected in the adjectives Steinbeck uses about him: 'his glance was ... calculating and pugnacious'. He seems ready for violence and is suspicious of Lennie and George, as the adverbs 'coldly' and 'gingerly' show.

He bends his arms and 'his hands closed into fists' as he goes into a 'crouch', which sounds like he is ready to attack someone. He is prepared for a fight and we learn later that he used to be a boxer.

To Kill a Mockingbird

Student A: Foundation Tier

When Scout falls over, she can hear Jem being attacked. There are 'scuffling, kicking sounds' and sounds of 'flesh scraping'. The worst is when she hears 'a dull crunching sound and Jem screamed'. Scout can't really help because she is trapped in her 'wire prison', which is a metaphor for the costume she is in.

Student B: Higher Tier

Scout never explains exactly what is happening because she is in costume and it is too dark to see so the author uses the effects of sound to present most of the violence. We share her fear of the unknown when the writer uses alliteration to describe suspicious sounds: 'swish' and 'wheek, wheek'.

> After Jem and Scout have stopped to listen, the writer breaks the suspense by having Jem scream 'Run, run' which adds to the sense of danger and urgency.
>
> At first, there are only natural obstacles that could hurt them ('stumping a toe') but now it is their attacker and the costumes they are wearing. Verbs like 'crushed', 'floundering' and 'entangled' and the metaphor of 'wire prison' suggest how Scout is helpless to protect against violence from their attacker.

Foundation Tier

Band	Description
1	• Basic understanding of how the writer uses language to present ideas • Limited reference to the extract to support response
2	• Some understanding of how the writer uses language to present ideas • Some reference to the extract to support response
3	• Generally sound or sound understanding of how the writer uses language to present ideas • Clear reference to the extract to support response

Higher Tier

Band	Description
1	• Mostly sound understanding of how the writer uses language to present ideas • Clear reference to the extract to support response
2	• Thorough understanding of how the writer uses language to present ideas to the reader • Sustained reference to the extract to support response
3	• Perceptive understanding of how the writer uses language to present ideas to the reader • Discriminating reference to the extract to support response

ResultsPlus
Build your skills

Fill in the RAG table below to see how your confidence has improved in the following areas:

	R	A	G
I can recognise the language features that writers use to create effects	○	○	○
I can identify language features from the extract which are relevant to use in my answer	○	○	○
I can comment on the effect of the language features identified in order to support my answer	○	○	○
I can put together all the points to write a clear answer	○	○	○

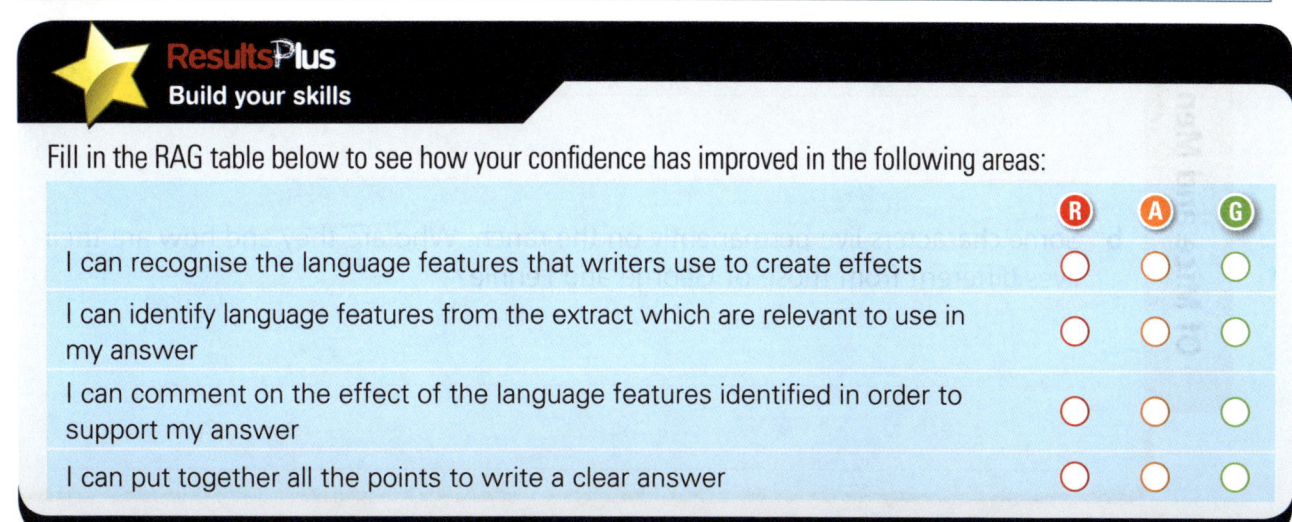

6 Answering questions on themes and context

I need to:
- show that I understand the themes within the text
- comment on how the theme relates to the context of the text.

In this section of the examination, **part (c)** of the question will ask you to comment on the significance of an idea, theme, relationship or a character's behaviour in an extract that you choose. You must also refer to the context of the text in your response. If you are taking the Foundation Tier paper, you will be given two bullet points which you must cover in your response in order to meet all the criteria against which you will be assessed.

ResultsPlus
Build your skills

Fill in the RAG table below to show how confident you are in the following areas:

	R	A	G
I know enough about themes to pick a section from the text which is relevant to the question set	○	○	○
I can explain how the theme is presented within the section of the text I have chosen	○	○	○
I can make reference to other parts of the text where necessary to explain the significance of the theme in the section of the text I have chosen	○	○	○
I can refer to the social and cultural context of the text in my answer	○	○	○

Activity 1

This activity will help you explore the context of the text you have studied.

10 MINS

1 Answer the following questions on your chosen text which will help you to start thinking about how the context is relevant when thinking about a relationship, idea or theme within an extract. You will not get questions like this in your examination.

Of Mice and Men

a   George and Lennie are itinerant workers. What does this mean and how does this affect how George and Lennie have to live their lives?

b   Some characters live permanently on the ranch. Who are they and how are their lives different from those of George and Lennie?

46

English Unit 2 | *Section B: Different Cultures*

c Curley's wife is seen as different from other characters on the ranch. Why is this? Give some examples of how this affects the events in the novel.

To Kill a Mockingbird

a Many white people in Maycomb County consider black people to be inferior to whites. Find some examples/evidence from the novel that show this attitude.

b Boo Radley is treated as an outsider in Maycomb. Who are the other outsiders in the novel? Why are they outsiders?

c The Ewells are referred to as 'white trash'. Why do people call them this? Are they seen as inferior to black people? Explain your answer.

6 Answering questions on themes and context

Activity 2

20 MINS

In part (c) of the examination, you need to choose your own extract to help you answer the question. This means that you need to know the text very well.

1 Look back at the extract you studied for Activity 3 in Lesson 2, on pages 42–43. Write a list of three different extracts from the text you could use to answer the sample examination question below that is relevant to your text and tier. Remember you may not choose the extract you looked at in Lesson 2 as one of your sections.

Of Mice and Men

Foundation Tier

Explain the importance of Curley's aggressive behaviour towards others on the ranch in **one other** part of the novel.

In your answer you **must** consider:
- how the writer describes Curley's aggressive behaviour
- how Curley's aggressive behaviour affects others. (10 marks)

Higher Tier

Explore the significance of Curley's aggressive behaviour towards others on the ranch in **one other** part of the novel.

You **must** refer to Curley's status on the ranch in your answer.

(10 marks)

To Kill a Mockingbird

Foundation Tier

Explain the importance of violence in **one other** part of the novel.

In your answer you **must** consider:
- why the violent incident takes place
- the effect of the violence on other people. (10 marks)

Higher Tier

Explore the significance of violence in **one other** part of the novel.

You **must** refer to the context of the novel in your answer.

(10 marks)

1 _____

2 _____

3 _____

The assessment objectives for part (c) require you to:
- comment on the writer's ideas and how he or she presents them
- show understanding of the context of the text when commenting on the significance of the idea, theme or relationship.

48

English Unit 2 | *Section B: Different Cultures*

If you are taking the Foundation Tier paper, two bullet points will be included in the question to help you to focus your answer. You must respond to both of these in order to get good marks.

If you are taking the Higher Tier paper, no bullet points will be included. You will need to 'explore' rather than 'explain' how an idea, theme or relationship is presented, which involves thinking further about the significance of the subject you have been asked about and putting forward a variety of ideas. You will also be given instructions on what you must cover in your answer (points relating to the context of the text), so try to ensure you follow these in order to get good marks.

2   Choose one of the extracts from the text in your list and re-read it.

Answer the following questions to help you think about the importance of the theme within the extract. You will not get questions like this in the examination.

   a   How does the writer present this incident/event? How does the writer make us feel about it?

   _____
   _____
   _____
   _____

   b   Why is the incident/event important in the text as a whole? Does it affect what happens next? Does it affect the characters?

   _____
   _____
   _____
   _____

   c   What does it tell us about the context of the text? Does it tell us something about the way people lived at the time? Does it tell us something about people's attitudes at the time?

   _____
   _____
   _____
   _____

49

6 Answering questions on themes and context

Activity 3

1 Read through the extract from your text specified below. In the examination, you will have an extract printed for you in its entirety. Then look at the sample part (c) examination question which requires you to write an answer based on **one other** extract from the text you have studied. You will need to choose an appropriate extract yourself.

(20 MINS)

Of Mice and Men, Section 5, pages 92–93

Read through the extract which appears at the start of Section 5. It starts as shown below, and ends with the words 'He rocked himself back and forth in his sorrow.'

> Only Lennie was in the barn, and Lennie sat in the hay beside a packing case under a manger in the end of the barn that had not been filled with hay. Lennie sat in the hay and looked at a little dead puppy that lay in front of him.

Foundation Tier

Many of the characters in *Of Mice and Men* are angry.

Explain the importance of anger in **one other** part of the novel.

In your answer you **must** consider:
- why the character or characters involved are angry
- how their anger affects others (10 marks)

Higher Tier

Many of the characters in *Of Mice and Men* are angry.

Explore the significance of anger in **one other part** of the novel.

You **must** refer to the context of the novel in your answer.

(10 marks)

To Kill a Mockingbird, Chapter 10, pages 103–104

Read through the extract which appears at the end of Chapter 10. It starts as shown below, and ends with the words "People in their right minds never take pride in their talents,' said Miss Maudie.'

> Jem became vaguely articulate: ''d you seem him, Scout? 'd you see him just standin' there?... 'n' all of a sudden he just relaxed all over, an' it looked like that gun was a part of him … an' he did it so quick, like … I hafta aim for ten minutes 'fore I can hit somethin'…'

Foundation Tier

In the extract, Scout learns about her father and his life in Maycomb County.

Explain what the reader learns about life in Maycomb County in **one other** part of the novel.

In your answer, you **must** consider:
- how the reader learns about life in Maycomb County
- why life in Maycomb County is important in the novel.

(10 marks)

Higher Tier

In the extract, Scout learns about her father and his life in Maycomb County.

Explore the significance of what the reader learns about life in Maycomb County in **one other** part of the novel.

You **must** refer to the context of the novel in your answer.

(10 marks)

50

English Unit 2 | *Section B: Different Cultures*

2 Choose the extract you will use to answer this question and write your response below. Remember to comment on the context of the text in your answer.

51

ResultsPlus
Build better answers

1 Read the student response to the sample examination question from Activity 2 relating to your text and tier.

Using the mark schemes opposite, decide which band the answer would achieve. Write an explanation of your decision.

I think the student would obtain a Band _____ because _____

_____

Of Mice and Men

Student A: Foundation Tier

We always see Curley behaving aggressively in the novel. He is constantly on the lookout to cause trouble and, although he has a fairly easy life, he does not seem very happy. An example of this is when George, Candy and Lennie have been discussing their plans to buy a farm. Curley, Slim and Carlson come back into the bunkhouse and Curley suspects them of seeing his wife. He threatens Carlson but Carlson is not scared and says he will 'kick his goddam head off'. This is unusual because Curley is the boss's son and he expects to be treated with respect. Lennie is an easy target because he is not a permanent worker on the farm and is simple-minded, but to Curley's surprise he fights back and crushes Curley's hand. Now, Curley bears a grudge against Lennie.

Student B: Higher Tier

Steinbeck makes the tragic outcome of the novel inevitable by showing how a series of small events lead to the destruction of George and Lennie's dream and the death of Lennie. A major factor in all this is the aggressive behaviour of Curley. This would not be so important if Curley was not the boss's son who jealously guards his superior status on the ranch. He cannot bear to see his wife flirt with other men and he cannot stand someone like Lennie, an itinerant worker and therefore one of the lowest of the low, making him. This is exactly what seems to be happening in the scene which leads to Lennie crushing his hand.

To Kill a Mockingbird

Student A: Foundation Tier

Tom Ewell beats his daughter Mayella because he saw her with Tom Robinson. This leads to Tom's arrest for attempted rape, something that horrified white people living in Maycomb County. The people of the town are willing to execute Tom even without a trial and he is found guilty even though he is innocent. This violence shows that racial prejudice is unfair and people can't face the truth when they suffer from it. Obviously, Tom is affected by it because he is put in prison and is killed trying to escape.

Student B: Higher Tier

> The most important act of violence in the novel is an invented one. Mayella's accusation that Tom Robinson assaulted her so that she can save face with her father is presented as part of her testimony in court. Harper Lee uses this lie to demonstrate how black people were treated in places like Maycomb in America in the 1930s. No-one likes the Ewells because they are thought of as white trash but when it comes to the crunch, even this will not overcome people's prejudices that a black man should not touch a white woman. Atticus does as much as he can to prove that Tom was innocent but nothing will stop the white population from closing ranks and finding him guilty.

Foundation Tier

Band	Description
1	• Basic understanding of theme and its importance in one other part of the novel. • Basic reference to the novel's context
2	• Some understanding of theme and its importance in one other part of the novel. • Some reference to the novel's context
3	• Generally sound or sound understanding of theme and its importance in one other part of the novel • Generally sound or sound reference to the novel's context

Higher Tier

Band	Description
1	• Generally sound or sound understanding of theme and its importance in one other part of the novel • Generally sound or sound reference to the novel's context
2	• Thorough understanding of theme and its importance in one other part of the novel • Sustained reference to the novel's context
3	• Perceptive understanding of theme and its importance in one other part of the novel • Discriminating reference to the novel's context

ResultsPlus
Build your skills

Fill in the RAG table below to see how your confidence has improved in the following areas:

	R	A	G
I know enough about themes to pick a section from the text which is relevant to the question set	○	○	○
I can explain how the theme is presented within the section of the text I have chosen	○	○	○
I can make reference to other parts of the text where necessary to explain the significance of the theme in the section of the text I have chosen	○	○	○
I can refer to the social and cultural context of the text in my answer	○	○	○

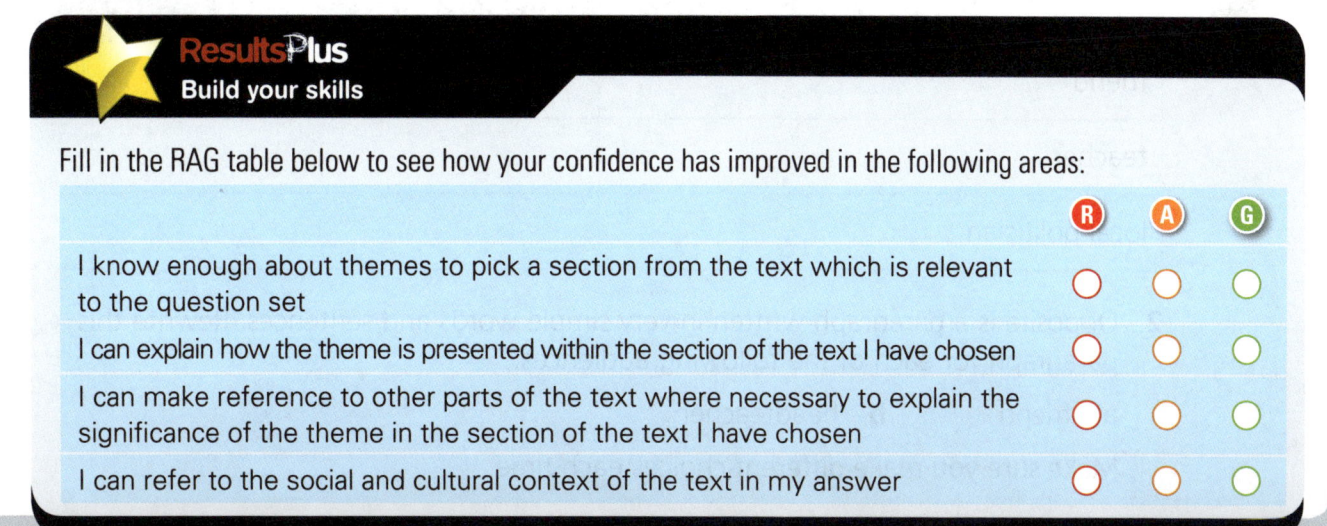

7 Making the right decisions

I need to:
- understand how to write for audience and purpose
- choose the most appropriate ideas for the audience and purpose.

This lesson will help you to make the right choices in your writing for Section C of the English examination. In the examination you will be given a choice of two questions, both of which will include instructions for your writing. You will need to answer *one* of the two questions. This lesson will help you revise what to do in response to the instructions in the question you choose.

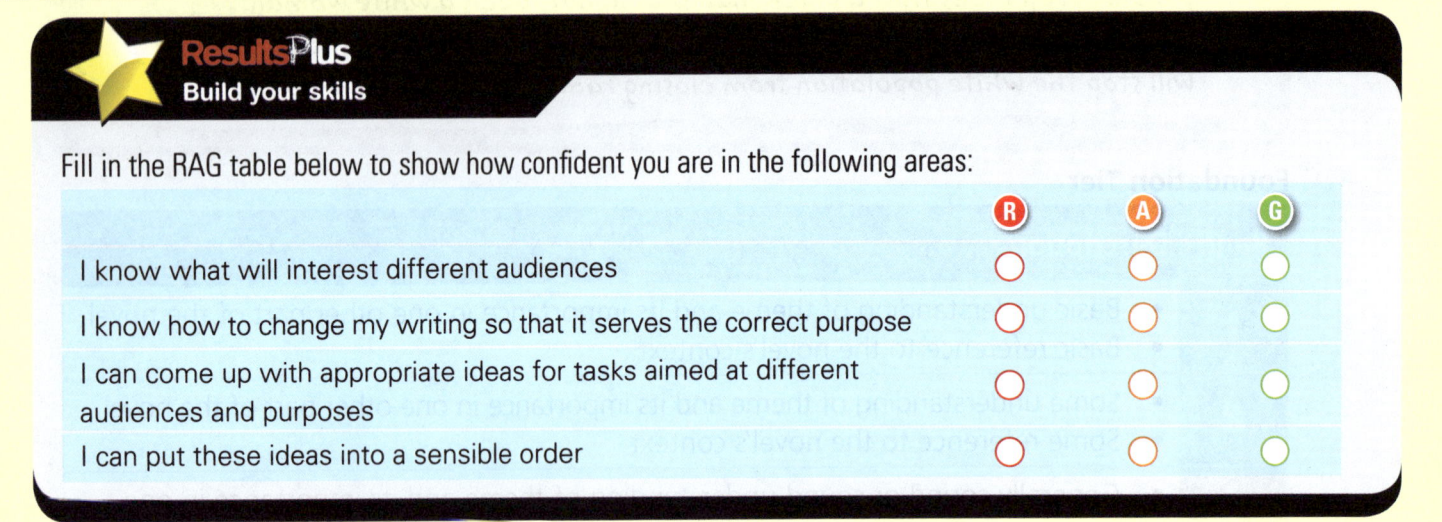

ResultsPlus: Build your skills

Fill in the RAG table below to show how confident you are in the following areas:

	R	A	G
I know what will interest different audiences	○	○	○
I know how to change my writing so that it serves the correct purpose	○	○	○
I can come up with appropriate ideas for tasks aimed at different audiences and purposes	○	○	○
I can put these ideas into a sensible order	○	○	○

Activity 1

You have to make choices depending on the **audience** for the piece of writing.

1. Complete the table below showing what you understand about the needs of the audience. You might want to use some of the words in the box to help you (they can each be used more than once).

> funny   formal   informal   chatty
> referring to shared experiences
> an impressive vocabulary   longer sentences   technical vocabulary

Audience	Language choice
friend	
teacher	
local politician	

2. Opposite is a paragraph written in very simple words and sentences. Rewrite this paragraph for each of the following audiences:

   a friend   b headteacher

   Make sure you make different choices each time.

54

English Unit 2 | *Section C: Writing*

> When I get home from school I do my homework. It is important I get it done straight away. I find a lot of homework easy and I do not learn very much. Homework just takes up a lot of my time. I would like to be practising the guitar. I would also like to be riding at the local stables.

a friend

b headteacher

3 List the differences between the paragraphs you have written. Explain why you made these different choices.

55

7 Making the right decisions

You also have to make different choices depending on the **purpose** of the piece of writing.

Activity 2

1 Complete these sentences:

   a When I persuade I am trying to…

   _____

   b To review something I must…

   _____

   c When I am writing to argue I need to…

   _____

   d Commenting on something means I must…

   _____

   e When I am exploring an idea or issue I should…

   _____

2 The following phrases have been written with one of the above purposes in mind. Label them with the most appropriate purpose.

   a It is easy to see why homework is important. However, there are many reasons why it might be considered a waste of time. _____

   b Homework is something that causes me great emotional turmoil. What is the point other than to upset me? _____

   c The current homework project is very successful. The choices that we were given helped to find something that was useful and interesting. _____

   d Homework is something that always causes difficulty, no matter which school you look at. _____

   e Overall, in my opinion, homework is something that has to be done. _____

Coming up with ideas is the most difficult part of the examination. You need to get really good at analysing the question to help you come up with ideas to write about. You need to think about the audience, purpose and subject of the piece of writing.

Look at this sample examination question, in which notes about the appropriate audience, purpose and subject are given. Remember that suggestions for things to include in your answer will *not* be given in the Higher Tier examination.

Purpose: give a broad overview of the subject and cover different perspectives. Some personal opinion.

Write an article for a lifestyle magazine in which you discuss the benefits and drawbacks of modern technology.

You may wish to include:

- details of how we use modern technology
- details about how modern technology has improved our lives
- what harmful effects modern technology might have
- any other ideas you may have.   (48 marks)

Audience: people who want to read about subjects that directly affect them on an everyday basis

Subject: how we use technology and give everyday examples of where it has a positive effect and where it has a negative effect

3 Now look at this sample examination question. Label the audience, purpose and subject and use them to come up with ideas in the same way.

Write an article for a teenage magazine in which you argue for or against the value of reality TV programmes.

- Possible reasons for their popularity.
- Possible benefits and possible negatives of reality TV programmes.
- your own opinions of reality TV programmes.
- any other ideas you may have.   (48 marks)

7 Making the right decisions

Activity 3

20 MINS You might find it useful to produce a spider diagram to help you come up with ideas. You should put the subject in the central circle and come up with as many ideas as possible, no matter how silly.

Look at this example:

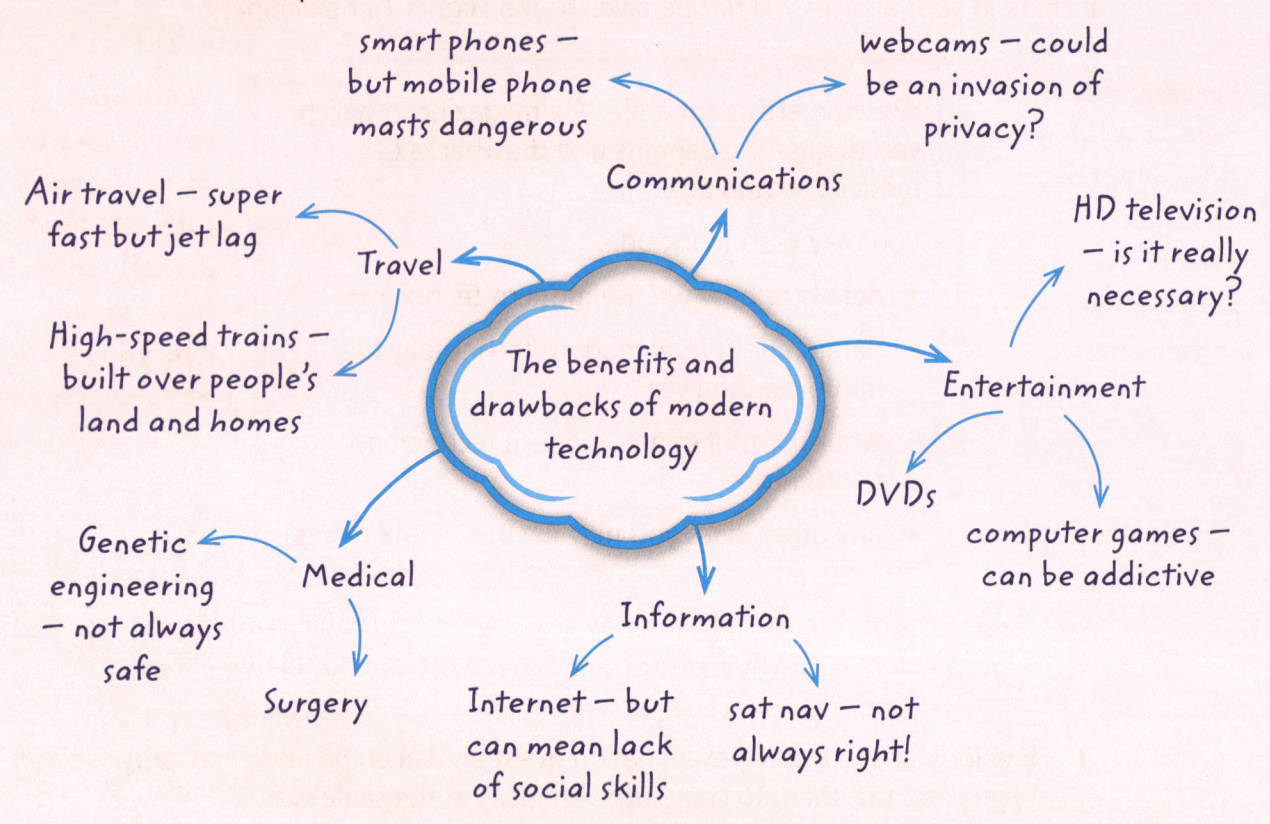

Spider diagram — central topic: The benefits and drawbacks of modern technology

- **Communications**
  - smart phones — but mobile phone masts dangerous
  - webcams — could be an invasion of privacy?
- **Travel**
  - Air travel — super fast but jet lag
  - High-speed trains — built over people's land and homes
- **Entertainment**
  - HD television — is it really necessary?
  - DVDs
  - computer games — can be addictive
- **Medical**
  - Genetic engineering — not always safe
  - Surgery
- **Information**
  - Internet — but can mean lack of social skills
  - sat nav — not always right!

1 Look at the spider diagram above for the article on modern technology. Remember the purpose is to discuss and the audience is people who want to read about subjects that directly affect them. Sort through the ideas and complete this table:

Good idea for the audience	Good idea because it will help text fulfil its purpose	Do not include

English Unit 2 | *Section C: Writing*

2 Now produce a spider diagram for the sample examination question from Question 3 in Activity 2 on page 57. Don't worry too much when you are producing your spider diagram. Write all your ideas down. Then, you should look through your ideas and select the ones that are most appropriate to the audience and purpose you have been given.

3 Now complete this table, selecting the ideas that are most appropriate for the audience and purpose of the question.

	Good idea for the audience	Good idea because it will help text fulfil its purpose	Do not include

59

ResultsPlus
Build better answers

Once you have come up with your ideas, you need to decide in which order to write about them.

1 You are going to use the ideas for the article on modern technology on page 58. You might want to use the ideas you came up with in Question 3 in Activity 3 on page 59 instead.

a Put the ideas into an order that seems sensible.

_____

_____

_____

_____

b Explain why the order you have come up with is sensible. You might want to start your explanation with:

This idea is best to go first because...

_____

_____

_____

_____

The process that you have completed in this lesson is as follows:
- Look closely at the question
- Come up with ideas
- Identify appropriate ideas
- Put your ideas in order

This process will help you to:
- come up with effective ideas
- organise your ideas into paragraphs.

You will be marked on your ability to do both of these things.

2 Look at the plans opposite for the sample examination question from page 57. Each student has come up with different ideas and put them into a different order in their plan.

60

Plan 1	Plan 2	Plan 3
1 Reality TV is great 2 X-Factor 3 Why it is great 4 The next series and people's concerns	1 What is reality TV? 2 Why people like it 3 Why people think it is bad 4 Overall, my opinion — ok sometimes	1 Story about what they involve — give specific examples 2 The variety of attitudes to reality TV and why it is popular 3 Good and bad points — give specific examples 4 My opinion is...

Decide which plan you think would get the best mark and explain your choice.

I think Plan _____ would get the best mark because _____

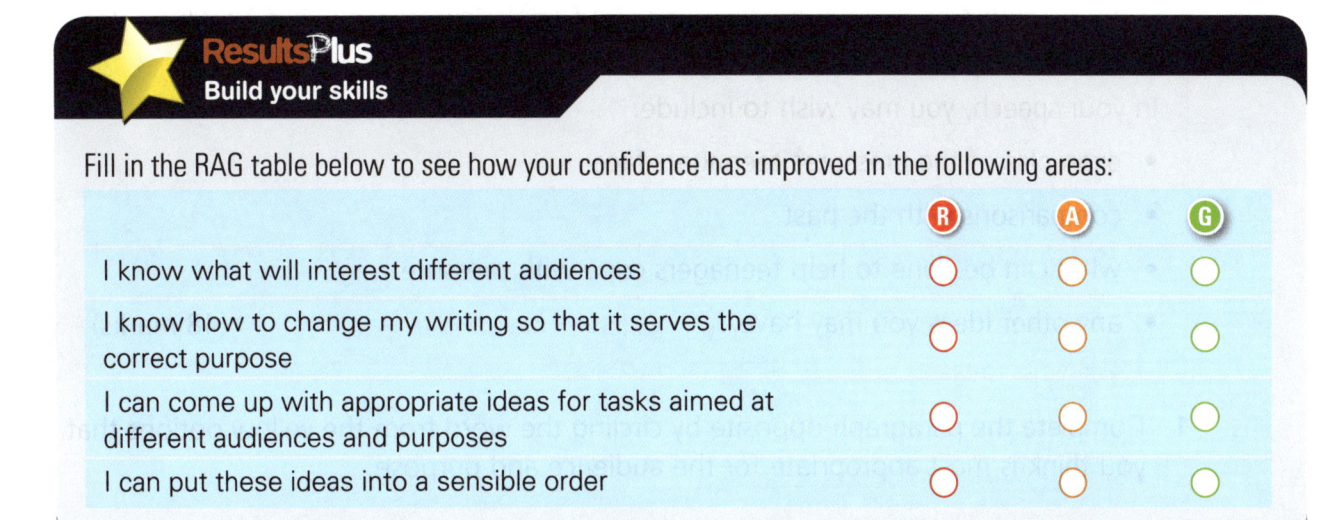

_____

_____

_____

_____

ResultsPlus
Build your skills

Fill in the RAG table below to see how your confidence has improved in the following areas:

	R	A	G
I know what will interest different audiences	○	○	○
I know how to change my writing so that it serves the correct purpose	○	○	○
I can come up with appropriate ideas for tasks aimed at different audiences and purposes	○	○	○
I can put these ideas into a sensible order	○	○	○

8 Choosing the right word

I need to:
- choose words that are appropriate for the audience and the purpose
- choose words that will interest my audience
- check that these words are spelt correctly.

This lesson will help you to choose words that will make your writing as interesting as possible. It is important to select words that are appropriate for your audience and purpose but it is crucial to engage your reader with clever choices.

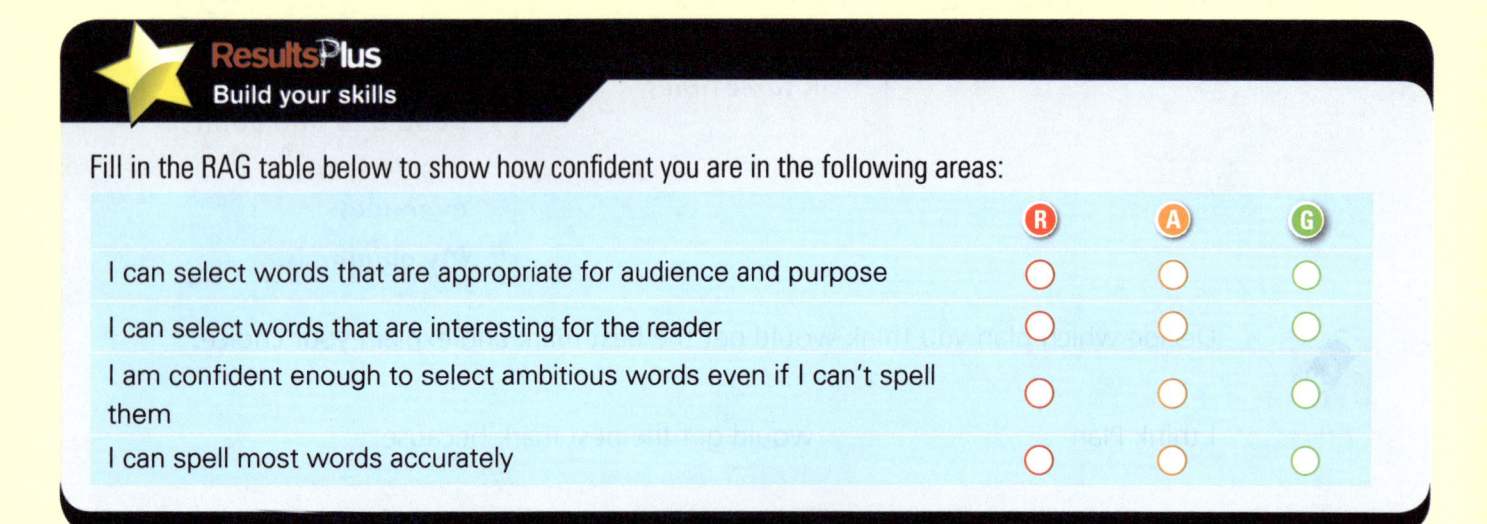

ResultsPlus
Build your skills

Fill in the RAG table below to show how confident you are in the following areas:

	R	A	G
I can select words that are appropriate for audience and purpose	○	○	○
I can select words that are interesting for the reader	○	○	○
I am confident enough to select ambitious words even if I can't spell them	○	○	○
I can spell most words accurately	○	○	○

Activity 1

(15 MINS)

It is important to select words that are appropriate to the audience.

Here is a sample examination question:

> Write the text for a speech for parents in which you attempt to persuade them that there are many pressures on teenagers today.
>
> In your speech, you may wish to include:
> - examples of the pressures teenagers face
> - comparisons with the past
> - what can be done to help teenagers cope with pressure
> - any other ideas you may have.   (48 marks)

1. Complete the paragraph opposite by circling the word from the yellow options that you think is most appropriate for the audience and purpose.

English Unit 2 | *Section C: Writing*

Your kids'/children's/teenagers' experience is incredibly/very different to what you lived through just a few years ago. Each day they are pushed/pressured/encouraged to work and behave in certain ways that you most likely have never imagined/believed/considered. School is all about results, friends are all about the right code of behaviour and family is about being cared for whilst looking mature/grown up/independent. There is no place where your kids/children/teenagers can relax, as they are always being judged/tested/pressured.

2 Here is another sample examination question. Remember that suggestions for things to include in your answer will *not* be given in the Higher Tier examination.

> Write a letter to a friend in which you review a film they have said they would like to see.
>
> In your email, you may wish to include:
> - basic details of the story
> - information about the camera-work or acting
> - whether or not you think they should go to see it
> - any other ideas you may have.   (48 marks)

Complete this paragraph by choosing words that you think are appropriate for the audience and purpose.

_____ John

I hear you would like to _____ the film Avatar! The film is _____ . It is about some marines who are stealing resources from a planet called Pandora. The story is _____ , John, you are maybe going to find it a little _____ . However, the _____ are _____ . You will love the way that you seem to fly through the air with the aliens. It is _____ .

3 Explain the differences in the choice of words between the speech to parents and the email to a friend.

8 Choosing the right word

Activity 2

15 MINS

You need to select a variety of words to keep your text interesting for the reader.

1 Here is another paragraph from the review of the film *Avatar*. It is reviewing the actors in the film.

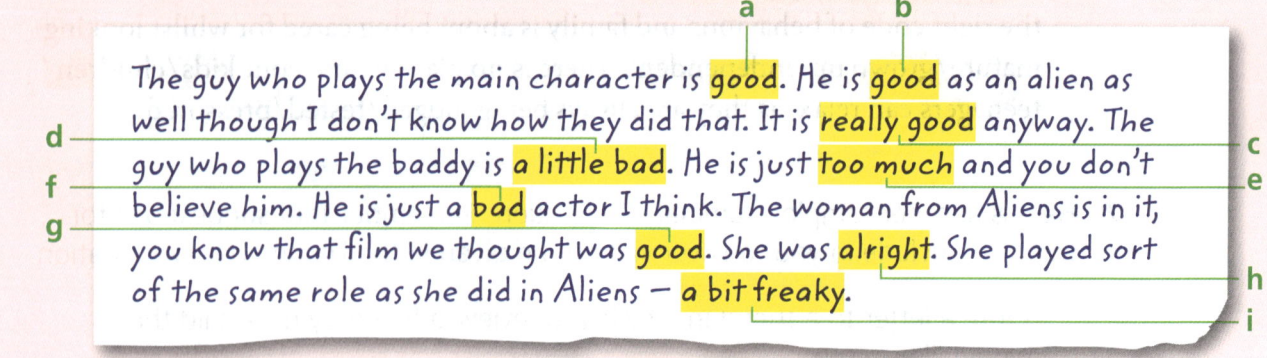

> The guy who plays the main character is **good**. He is **good** as an alien as well though I don't know how they did that. It is **really good** anyway. The guy who plays the baddy is **a little bad**. He is just **too much** and you don't believe him. He is just a **bad** actor I think. The woman from Aliens is in it, you know that film we thought was **good**. She was **alright**. She played sort of the same role as she did in Aliens – **a bit freaky**.

a — good
b — good
c — too much
d — really good
e — alright
f — a little bad
g — bad
h — good
i — a bit freaky

Change the highlighted words or phrases. Use words or phrases that would offer more information to the reader. For instance, instead of 'a little bad' you might say 'poor', which is a more accurate use of words.

My alternative words:

a _____

b _____

c _____

d _____

e _____

f _____

g _____

h _____

i _____

64

2 Choose words that show the examiner that you have an extensive vocabulary. You might know the perfect word but you might not know how to use it within a sentence.

Here are some words that you could have used in the paragraph about the actors that might entertain the reader more.

intense	sensitive	exaggerated
emotive	convincing	unconvincing
passable	talented	

Rewrite the paragraph using these words. You can use other words if you think you have better ones. Be adventurous in your choice of words!

8 Choosing the right word

Activity 3

You will get some marks for spelling. Don't worry too much if you find it hard to spell more difficult words correctly; just make sure that you are careful to spell the easier words that you do know correctly.

1 Look through some of your exercise books from school. Make a list of all the words that your teacher has marked as being spelt incorrectly.

_____

_____

_____

_____

_____

2 Look closely at this list of most commonly misspelt words:

address	guarantee	occurrence
advice	harass	piece
beginning	humorous	prejudice
believe	independent	privilege
changeable	jealous	receive
conscientious	knowledge	rhythm
conscious	leisure	separate
deceive	library	sincerely
definite	mediocre	special
desperate	miniature	surprise
disastrous	miscellaneous	thorough
embarrass	mischievous	through
fascinate	mysterious	truly
fiery	necessary	until
government	neighbour	weird
grateful	occasion	

English Unit 2 | *Section C: Writing*

    a Highlight any interesting words that you think you would be able to use in a piece of writing.

    b Tick any word that you know you can spell.

    c Add any word that is not ticked to the list that you created in Question 1.

3 Choose a word from the list in Question 2 that you would not normally use. Try to write a sentence using the word. Check the meaning in the dictionary if you are not sure. Repeat the process for two other words on the list.

1

2

3

4 Produce a bookmark and write all the words that you need to pay special attention to onto one side of the bookmark. Use the bookmark in a book that you use all the time.

ResultsPlus
Build better answers

15 MINS Here is the sample examination question again. Remember that suggestions for things to include in your answer will *not* be given in the Higher Tier examination.

> Write a letter to a friend in which you review a film they have said they would like to see.
>
> In your email, you may wish to include:
> - basic details of the story
> - information about the camera-work or acting
> - whether or not you think they should go to see it
> - any other ideas you may have. (48 marks)

1 Write the opening paragraph in response to this question, reviewing a film you have watched. You should focus on the words that you choose.

_____

_____

_____

_____

_____

_____

_____

2 Read your paragraph. Use different coloured pens to highlight or underline:

  a words you are proud of

  b words that you think are not appropriate for the audience or purpose

  c words that you think could be replaced with something more interesting

  d words that you think are spelt incorrectly.

3 Make changes to your paragraph.

  a Change words so that they are more appropriate and more entertaining.

  b Change words that you think are spelt incorrectly. Listen to the sound of the word and make another attempt.

ResultsPlus
Build your skills

Fill in the RAG table below to see how your confidence has improved in the following areas:

	R	A	G
I can select words that are appropriate for audience and purpose	○	○	○
I can select words that are interesting for the reader	○	○	○
I am confident enough to select ambitious words even if I can't spell them	○	○	○
I can spell most words accurately	○	○	○

9 Choosing sentences

I need to:
- write sentences that are appropriate to audience and purpose
- write sentences that are interesting for the reader
- remember to use correct punctuation.

This lesson will help you to write in sentences. It is obviously important to use punctuation in your sentences but you need to be able to use punctuation so that it has an impact on your audience. This lesson will also help you to write appropriate and interesting sentences.

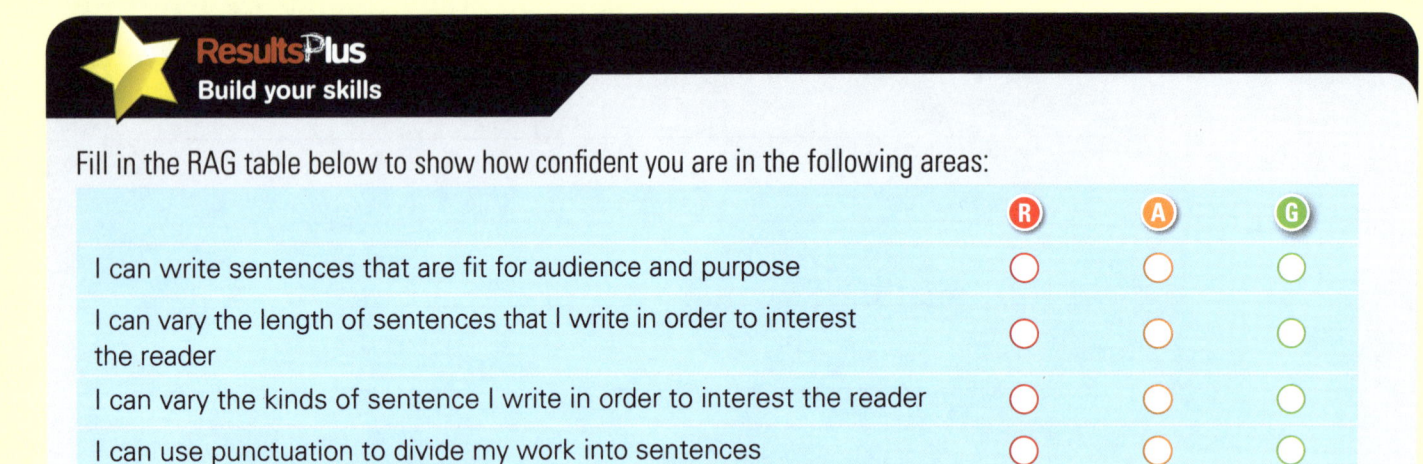

ResultsPlus
Build your skills

Fill in the RAG table below to show how confident you are in the following areas:

	R	A	G
I can write sentences that are fit for audience and purpose	○	○	○
I can vary the length of sentences that I write in order to interest the reader	○	○	○
I can vary the kinds of sentence I write in order to interest the reader	○	○	○
I can use punctuation to divide my work into sentences	○	○	○
I can use punctuation to add meaning to my work	○	○	○

Activity 1

At the most basic level you should be careful to put full stops and capital letters in your work. You should practise checking your work.

20 MINS

1 Here is a paragraph where no sentences have been marked. Insert full stops and capital letters.

school uniform is meant to make life easier for students they are less

likely to get bullied and they don't have to buy expensive clothes however

there is the cost of uniform and the fact that people deserve to have

some choice in what they wear some schools try to balance uniform and

students' own clothes by wearing a casual top but all this does is make

English Unit 2 | *Section C: Writing*

people look untidy it seems that there is no easy answer when it comes

to school uniform

2   You also need to be able to use other types of punctuation. The mark scheme asks you to use a variety of punctuation. You need to try to use question marks, exclamation marks and commas.
Complete these sentences with the appropriate punctuation:

a   Why do headteachers insist on school uniform

b   It is not true

c   Wearing uniform does not prevent bullying as any student will tell you people are still capable of making you feel different even when you look the same

3   Rewrite the paragraph about school uniform from Question 1. Include the different sentences you have just completed.

_____
_____
_____
_____
_____
_____

4   Read the paragraph with only full stops in Question 1. Now read the paragraph with the new sentences that include a question mark, exclamation mark and some commas in Question 3. How do they change the 'feel' of the writing?

_____
_____
_____

71

9 Choosing sentences

Activity 2

In the examination, you need to write in a way that is suitable for the audience and purpose. To make your writing interesting, you should try to vary the kinds of sentence you use. Here are some tips:

Exclamations

These are sentences that end in an exclamation mark.

- Exclamations can be used to emphasise a point – but don't use them too often.
- Exclamations can be used to show that you think something is surprising or amazing.
- *Don't* use these in very formal pieces of writing.
- *Do* use these in informal writing.

Questions

These are sentences that end in a question mark. If the person reading is not actually going to answer the question (e.g. if it is in a newspaper article) it is called a **rhetorical question**.

- Use rhetorical questions to get the reader to think about an issue.
- Rhetorical questions engage the reader's interest and can make your writing more interesting.
- Rhetorical questions are very useful when you are writing to persuade or to argue.

Sentence length

It is a good idea to vary the length of your sentences. This will make your writing flow better.

- Use a short sentence after a long sentence to emphasise a point.
- If you use long sentences, check you have included correct punctuation.

1. Read the tips above. Now look at the extract below. It has been written to argue that school uniform is a good thing.

> Most teenagers are interested in fashion and like to express themselves through their clothes. But most schools still have school uniform. There are several reasons for this. If everybody has to wear the same clothes then nobody will pick on students who are less fashionable, or can't afford the latest clothes.

a Replace one of the sentences with a rhetorical question.

b Read the paragraph again and explain the effect of the rhetorical question on the writing as a whole.

2 Read the paragraph below. It is the opening paragraph of an article in a teenage magazine reviewing the fitness activities available to young people in the town of Holmethorpe. The audience is young people in the local area.

> Sometimes it seems like there's not much to do, but actually Holmethorpe is packed full of surprising activities if you look for them. Whenever you next feel bored, check out the local sports club which runs all kinds of classes from football to dance and from cross-country to boules. Even javelin-throwing is on the agenda. If you're feeling very adventurous take a visit to the climbing wall where you can get a reduced young-person rate for an hour of clambering with a personal instructor. Guaranteed to get you active.

a Add in an exclamation mark.

b Change the punctuation to vary the length of the sentences. You can change words if you need to do so.

c Read the new paragraph and explain the effect of the changes you have made.

73

9 Choosing sentences

Activity 3

20 MINS

To use sentences well you need to:
- use a variety of sentences – long and short, questions and exclamations
- use accurate punctuation.

Here is a sample examination question. Remember that suggestions for things to include in your answer will *not* be given in the Higher Tier examination.

> Write an article for the school website reviewing the facilities available to young people in your area.
>
> In your article, you may wish to include:
> - details about the facilities
> - quotes from people who use the facilities, giving their opinions
> - your own opinion about the facilities and ideas on improvements that could be made.
> - any other ideas you may have. (48 marks)

1. Write a paragraph in response to this examination question. Remember to think about the audience (students) and purpose (to review).

74

2 Read your paragraph again.

- Have you included sentences of different lengths?
- Could you include a rhetorical question?
- Could you include an exclamation? Is it appropriate?
- Is the writing appropriate for your audience (students)? Is it appropriate for the purpose (to review)?

Make changes to your paragraph below.

3 Re-read your paragraph. Is the punctuation accurate? Make any necessary corrections.

ResultsPlus
Build better answers

In the examination, you get some marks for being interesting and some marks for being accurate.

1 Read the following paragraphs. They are extracts from student answers to the sample examination question on page 78.

Student A

> The first performance of the school musical 'The Wiz' was on Friday. Over 70 people came to see the performance. The performance was in the school hall. Everybody thought it was really good. The audience really enjoyed the singing and dancing. Chantelle Pryce was brilliant as Dorothy. Andrea Furlong was also great as Aunt Em she had to play an old lady, which must have been difficult.

Student B

> On Friday, over 70 people came to see the first performance of 'The Wiz' in the school hall. Everybody thought it was excelent, and the audience seemed to particularly enjoy the singing and dancing. Chantelle Pryce was brilliant as Dorothy and Andrea Furlong was also great as Aunt Em. She had an especially tough role as she had to play an old lady!

a Can you spot any mistakes in the paragraphs? Highlight each one.

b Which paragraph do you think is more interesting? Explain your reasons.

Student _____'s paragraph is more interesting because _____

_____

_____

_____

2 Explain in your own words what you need to remember to do when writing and editing sentences.

_____

_____

_____

_____

ResultsPlus
Build your skills

Fill in the RAG table below to show how your confidence has improved in the following areas:

	R	A	G
I can write sentences that are fit for audience and purpose	○	○	○
I can vary the length of sentences that I write in order to interest the reader	○	○	○
I can vary the kinds of sentence I write in order to interest the reader	○	○	○
I can use punctuation to divide my work into sentences	○	○	○
I can use punctuation to add meaning to my work	○	○	○

10 Making best use of paragraphs

I need to:
- write in paragraphs
- link paragraphs together
- develop ideas within paragraphs.

This lesson will help you to organise your ideas within your writing. Once you have decided which ideas to include in your writing, you need to think of a basic paragraph structure. For each new idea you should use a new paragraph. Your job when you are writing is to make the ideas in these paragraphs clear and to make sure they all combine together to make one whole piece of writing.

ResultsPlus — Build your skills

Fill in the RAG table below to show how confident you are in the following areas:

	R	A	G
I know when to change paragraphs when I am writing	○	○	○
I understand how to link ideas between paragraphs	○	○	○
I know how to develop ideas within a paragraph	○	○	○

Activity 1

This activity will refresh your memory about what to do when you first enter the examination.

Here is a sample examination question. Remember that if you are taking the Higher Tier paper you will not be given the three bullet points.

> Write a review for the school magazine focused on a recent school event such as a sports team's performance or a recent production.
>
> In your review, you may wish to include:
> - a description of the event
> - anything significant that happened at the event
> - your own opinion about the event
> - any other ideas you may have.   (48 marks)

English Unit 2 | *Section C: Writing*

1. Label the question on page 78, making notes on the audience, purpose and subject of the piece of writing.

2. Now draw a spider diagram. Come up with as many ideas as you can.

3. List the four ideas you are going to use and the order in which you are going to write about them.

_____

_____

_____

_____

You now have the four topics for the four paragraphs you are going to write in your response to the examination question. This is called a paragraph map.

10 Making best use of paragraphs

Activity 2

Here is a sample examination question. Remember that suggestions for what to include in your answer will **not** be given in the Higher Tier examination.

> Write the text for a speech for parents in which you persuade them that they should support a charity you feel strongly about.
>
> In your speech you may wish to include:
> - information about what the charity does
> - why you think it is important
> - how parents can help
> - any other ideas you think are important. (48 marks)

Here is a sample paragraph map for this question:

Paragraph 1 Welcome the parents and explain why they have always been helpful in the past.

Paragraph 2 Give background to charity.

Paragraph 3 Explain why help is needed so much now.

Paragraph 4 Ask for their help and give examples how.

The best way to make sure the reader understands what the paragraph is going to be about is to use a topic sentence at the start of the paragraph. For instance:

I would like to welcome our generous parents to this charity event this evening.

1 Write a topic sentence for each of the remaining three paragraphs.

Topic sentence 2:

Topic sentence 3:

Topic sentence 4:

English Unit 2 | *Section C: Writing*

You then need to be able to develop the main idea of the paragraph by giving reasons, descriptions and examples. For instance:

An example — **Some description**

> I would like to welcome our generous parents to this charity event this evening. In the past you have always supported us fully in our aims and for this we are grateful. There was the huge effort when we chose to walk the length of the UK, thanks especially to the Jacksons for following me so closely with the van that served drinks! There was also the massive fair we held on the field that produced funds for the new sports centre. I know some of you parents have got much fitter thanks to this: so maybe not so selfless!

Another example — **A reason**

2. Write the second paragraph for this piece of writing. Develop the idea in the paragraph by giving reasons, descriptions and examples.

10 Making best use of paragraphs

Activity 3

20 MINS

You need to link your paragraphs together so that they flow to become one piece of writing. The easiest way to do this is to use connectives such as:

- firstly
- in conclusion
- also
- on the other hand
- however
- yet
- it could also be said

1   Rewrite your topic sentences from Activity 2 to include connectives. For instance:

> *However, more help is needed from you today!*

Topic sentence 2:
_____
_____

Topic sentence 3:
_____
_____

Topic sentence 4:
_____
_____

Another technique you can use is a question. For instance, at the end of the first paragraph shown on page 81 you could write:

> *So, you're thinking: what do they want us to do now?*

2   Use a question at the end of the second paragraph of the response you wrote in Activity 2 Question 2. Use the question to introduce the idea that is coming in the next paragraph.

_____
_____
_____

82

English Unit 2 | *Section C: Writing*

Finally, you can use key words at the beginning of the next paragraph that repeat ideas that have been used in the previous paragraph. For instance, the second paragraph could begin:

> *I am hoping the Jackson family are ready to follow me again as we take on an even bigger challenge than walking through the countryside!*

This helps to link and structure your writing effectively.

3 Write the third paragraph for this examination response below. Use key words from the second paragraph to help introduce ideas in this paragraph.

ResultsPlus
Build better answers

Here is a sample examination question:

> Write a letter to your local newspaper suggesting how your neighbourhood could be improved.
>
> In your letter you may wish to include:
> - reasons why your local area needs to be improved
> - your suggestions for improvements
> - how local people and the local area would benefit
> - any other ideas you may have. (48 marks)

1 a Label the question with notes on the content you will include that is appropriate for audience, purpose and subject.

b Create a spider diagram on a separate sheet of paper with further ideas.

c Draw up a paragraph map below.

Paragraph 1 _____

Paragraph 2 _____

Paragraph 3 _____

Paragraph 4 _____

2 Write the opening two paragraphs for your response to this question.

_____

_____

_____

_____

_____

_____

_____

_____

_____

3 Re-read your paragraphs and answer these questions:
   a Have I remembered to start each paragraph on a new line? ☐
   b Have I used topic sentences to introduce the key idea in the paragraph? ☐
   c Have I used examples, reasons and descriptions to develop ideas? ☐
   d Have I used connectives or key words to link the paragraphs? ☐
   e Have I used a question to help to introduce the idea in the next paragraph? ☐

ResultsPlus
Build your skills

Fill in the RAG table below to see how your confidence has improved in the following areas:

	R	A	G
I know when to change paragraphs when I am writing	○	○	○
I understand how to link ideas between paragraphs	○	○	○
I know how to develop ideas within a paragraph	○	○	○

Published by Pearson Education Limited, a company incorporated in England and Wales, having its registered office at Edinburgh Gate, Harlow, Essex, CM20 2JE. Registered company number: 872828

Edexcel is a registered trademark of Edexcel Limited

Text © Pearson Education Limited 2011

The rights of Racheal Smith and Keith Hurst to be identified as authors of this work have been asserted by them in accordance with the Copyright, Designs and Patent Act 1988.

First published 2011

15 14 13 12 11
10 9 8 7 6 5 4 3 2 1

British Library Cataloguing in Publication Data
A catalogue record for this book is available from the British Library

ISBN 978 1 846907 12 8

Copyright notice
All rights reserved. No part of this publication may be reproduced in any form or by any means (including photocopying or storing it in any medium by electronic means and whether or not transiently or incidentally to some other use of this publication) without the written permission of the copyright owner, except in accordance with the provisions of the Copyright, Designs and Patents Act 1988 or under the terms of a licence issued by the Copyright Licensing Agency, Saffron House, 6¬–10 Kirby Street, London EC1N 8TS (www.cla.co.uk). Applications for the copyright owner's written permission should be addressed to the publisher.

Designed and typeset by Juice Creative Limited, Hertfordshire
Printed and bound in Spain by Grafos S. A.

Picture Credits
Cover image: iStockphoto: Krzysztof Kwiatkowski

Acknowledgements
We would like to thank Tony Farrell and Polly Hennessy for their invaluable help in the development of this title.

We are grateful to the following for permission to reproduce copyright material:

Extracts pages 33 and 40 from *To Kill a Mockingbird* by Harper Lee, published by William Heinemann. Reprinted by permission of The Random House Group Ltd; Extracts pages 32 and 40 from *Of Mice and Men*, Copyright © John Steinbeck, 1937, 1965. Reproduced by permission of Penguin Books Ltd. From OF MICE AND MEN by John Steinbeck, copyright 1937, renewed © 1965 by John Steinbeck. Used by permission of Viking Penguin, a division of Penguin Group (USA) Inc.

Every effort has been made to contact copyright holders of material reproduced in this book and we apologise for any unintentional omissions. Any omissions will be rectified in subsequent printings if notice is given to the publishers.

Disclaimer
This material has been published on behalf of Edexcel and offers high-quality support for the delivery of Edexcel qualifications.

This does not mean that the material is essential to achieve any Edexcel qualification, nor does it mean that it is the only suitable material available to support any Edexcel qualification. Edexcel material will not be used verbatim in setting any Edexcel examination or assessment. Any resource lists produced by Edexcel shall include this and other appropriate resources.

Copies of official specifications for all Edexcel qualifications may be found on the Edexcel website: www.edexcel.com